WRESTLING WITH GOD

Lessons from the life of Jacob

D1339455

Wrestling with God

Lessons from the life of Jacob

J. DOUGLAS MACMILLAN

EVANGELICAL PRESS OF WALES

© Evangelical Press of Wales, 1991
First published 1991
First reprint 1994
ISBN 1 85049 091 0

This book is based on a series of addresses delivered at the Annual English Conference of the Evangelical Movement of Wales at Aberystwyth in August 1983.

Published by the Evangelical Press of Wales
Bryntirion, Bridgend, Mid Glamorgan, CF31 4DX
Printed by Mid Wales Litho, Pontypool, Gwent

Contents

Preface

Few who heard these sermons when they were preached at the Annual English Conference of the Evangelical Movement of Wales at Aberystwyth are likely to forget the impact they had at the time. Here was a diagnosis of spiritual need and a dimension of spiritual experience that was new to many. But as we heard these truths expounded they so evidently met the need of the times.

The former shepherd and wrestler, subsequently minister of the gospel and theological college professor, all combined to provide a wealth of vivid and powerful illustrations as the preacher opened up one of the treasure stores of God's Word.

Here is no trite handling of our present need of an experience of God. Nor is the necessity of prevailing with Him in prayer dealt with in the superficial manner so commonly found. Rather, there is a depth of insight, simply and often beautifully expressed, that makes the story of Jacob leap to life across the intervening centuries.

What Douglas MacMillan has succeeded so admirably in doing is to show us that far from being a character remote from us today in his problems, culture and trials, Jacob and his experiences at Bethel and Peniel are truly normative for the people of God in any age.

A generation of Christians like ours that feeds itself so often on Christian 'junk food' and as a result mistakes carnal excitement for the presence of the living God could do no better than to read and ponder the message of these pages. If we would learn what prayer really is, how vital it is and how God is able to meet and deal with men and women who seek Him, there is great help for us here.

I pray that the Lord who signally blessed the substance of these addresses when they were preached will again — and to an even greater degree — deign to add His further blessing to them as they appear in printed form.

Graham Harrison

1

'And he blessed him there'
(Genesis 32:29).

The story of Jacob's wrestling at Peniel is familiar to every reader of the Bible. It has often been the subject of meditation for Christian believers, and preachers and commentators have applied it in widely different ways to the lives of God's children. Yet it is always fresh and suggestive of new lessons for the spiritual life. Every time we come to it, whether in our private reading of Scripture or by instruction from the pulpit, it presents us with some of the fundamental features of the work of God in the soul of man. It would be correct to say that even the very young have heard it and read it many times, and each time with renewed interest. The explanation for this is simple: this ancient story makes a direct appeal to the very deepest realities in human life, and particularly to the profound workings of God's grace in the salvation of his people.

The narrative is recorded in Genesis 32:24-32, closing this fascinating chapter of Scripture, and providing a glimpse into one of the great mountain-top experiences in the life of this man of God. From the human standpoint it is the account of a man, alone with God in the dark of the night, facing the inward, hidden issues of the soul and made sharply aware of their presence and their power. It is not merely outward circumstances which trouble his mind, but the spiritual realities behind them. The pressures of life have set him apart and driven him to seek God in this way. Now events have conspired to add a note of urgency to his determination to fulfil this one great purpose of meeting with God.

On the divine side it is the story of how God, in covenant grace and mercy, worked in and through the circumstances of Jacob to bring him to this very place and this very hour. God was going to further his knowledge of his heart's sin and his heart's need, and he was going to lead him into a deep experience of divine goodness, divine favour, and divine sufficiency. It is the story of how God, or as he is often called in Genesis, the Angel of the Lord (cf. Genesis 16:7; 21:17; 22:11), who had made himself known to Jacob some twenty years earlier, stooped once more to touch his life. He comes to Jacob on his own level, appearing to him, laying hold of him, touching him, and moulding him. It is God coming, not merely in the form of man, but as the Man who in the fulness of time will come 'in the flesh' to live and die and atone for sin. It is the intrusion into the life of Jacob of the God of all grace, coming to enlighten, to humble, to change, to make himself known. In one way that is the whole of the story. In that same way, it is the story of every person who is pursued by God's grace and brought into God's family by the hand and the touch of Jesus Christ, himself the Angel of the covenant; for these are not two different beings but one and the same.

A POWERFUL ENCOUNTER

The passage provides us with a marvellous instance of encounter with God, and finds its focus in the theme of a power that transforms. That power is the saving power of God in the life of man. It is this power which makes the gospel the most significant thing in the world. From the human perspective it radically changes every life in which it works, and from the divine it brings to fruition the saving purpose of God through the redemptive work of Christ. The central factor in this encounter between God and Jacob is found in verse 29, 'And he blessed him there.' That phrase gives us the key to the entire incident, and we must not allow it to slip from our minds. Much happened to Jacob at Peniel, but the supreme and superb outcome was this; there God 'blessed' him.

That is why we gather at Christian conferences, or come together for Bible study, or read Christian books. We do those things in order to meet with God and to enjoy his blessing. That is what we look for in Christian worship, and Christian fellowship, and Christian service. It is what we pray for when we bring ourselves under the preaching of the Word, or when we seek God in the fellowship of prayer. We are, we say, seeking that 'the Lord will bless us'. When the Lord does bless us through those means, and others as well, then we cherish the experience and we never forget it. We cherish it even though there may have been pain and anguish and repentance in our souls, as the Lord brought us along to the place and hour of blessing. To have God's blessing outweighs all other considerations for the child of God. That is why verse 29 is so important, so critical, to our understanding of what took place at Peniel. 'He blessed him there.'

While we will not encounter God in the dramatic way that Jacob did, and must not look for such physical experiences, we can, nevertheless, encounter the same God and enjoy the same blessing and come under the same power as Jacob. The details and the circumstances are not likely to be repeated, but behind the details and events of Peniel we can trace the moral and the spiritual lessons, and see the lines in Jacob's life which all led up to the hour and place of blessing. There are enduring, unchanging, spiritual principles in God's saving, gracious dealings with his own people — elements and factors inherent in every saving blessing which comes to us from God. Those are the features of this story which we will attempt to draw out in the course of this book.

To know Jesus as Lord and Saviour is, of course, what makes one a Christian. That truth is basic, and so important that it underlies and undergirds everything which will come before us in these chapters. That God, through Christ and in Christ, breaks into men's lives, making himself known, binding their hearts to him, bringing their wills, their ways and their affections into the orbit of his gracious influence — that is the grandest fact in all the history and possibility of human experience. It is the reality which lies at the heart of this story.

A TRANSFORMING ENCOUNTER

The effect of such an encounter is incalculable. It uproots and changes everything in the life of its subjects. It is so integral a part of true Christian experience as to be one of its essential features, so that the apostle Paul describes a Christian in terms of its consequences: 'If any man be in Christ, he is a new creature: old things are passed away; behold, all things are become new' (2 Corinthians 5:17).

This transformation of human character involves not only God's power but his unmerited favour. That is part of what we call his grace. Here we have to reckon with one of the elementary facts that faced Jacob at Peniel. It is the fact that when God comes to deal with any man in mercy he comes to very unpromising material. The Bible makes that clear here as everywhere, and our human experience only verifies the truth of the Bible when we are honest enough to admit it — or even so stubborn as to deny it.

This feature of human life finds vivid illustration in the experience of Jacob. Like a great many others whom God has touched and saved, he is a man in whom we see much of the darkness and perversity that sin works in men. Yet the very sins and selfish wrongs in Jacob's life set out all the more wonderfully how free and undeserved is the mercy that the grace of God brings to him. In him the power that transforms is demonstrated to be so fully the gift of God's grace that his entire history is a graphic expression of the truth that 'where sin abounded, grace did much more abound' (Romans 5:20).

14

If ever there was a man who failed in the place of obedience and holiness that man was Jacob. How fitting then, that from the story of Jacob we learn and relearn that all-important lesson about the gospel method of a sinner's justification by God. We are saved not by works but by faith. From Jacob we are reminded that heaven is gained not by the endeavours of our own hearts but by the grace of God coming in renewing, regenerating, quickening power, making us new creatures in Christ Jesus.

Peniel is a place where the strands of Jacob's life are seen to meet in ways that wonderfully exhibit the grace of God. He had left home under sad and spiritually depressing circumstances more than twenty years earlier. His mother's impatience to hurry on the blessing of God for him, together with his own readiness to snatch at every seeming advantage, had meant estrangement from his ageing father Isaac, and ensured enmity from his twin brother Esau. By the time he arrives at Peniel, he has had twenty years with Laban — and it is questionable if there is a meaner man in the whole range of the Old Testament writings than the Laban of those years. The one good thing about Laban is that he throws Jacob into sharp relief! Twenty years with Laban explain a good deal of the way the natural guile of Jacob had hardened into pride and selfishness.

It is at this juncture, when those long years with their tests of faith, their trial of patience, and their erosion of humility are behind him, that a strange and rather frightening thing occurs. Just as he is about to step back into the land of youth and of God's promise Jacob is startled out of his joy, perhaps even his complacency, by hearing that Esau is coming to meet him accompanied by an army of four hundred men. Laban and Esau were the two men that Jacob need fear. Laban was no longer a threat, but here was Esau, and he must be faced. Jacob would need all his trickiness. The question was, would it be enough?

AN INSTRUCTIVE ENCOUNTER

Let there be no misunderstanding. Jacob was a tricky character. He had a high estimate of his own abilities, and his wits had served him well in the past. God had been good to him and Jacob knew that. He had been helped and blessed through the past twenty years in an extraordinary fashion. He could say to Laban, 'The Lord has blessed you because of me.' Yet, despite the goodness and tenderness and prosperity that God had showered upon him, he still had lessons to learn about trust and obedience. This encounter, taking place at the very border of the Promised Land as he was about to enter it after all those years, was to have a powerful and lasting effect on his life.

Before entering into an examination of the passage itself, it is necessary to acknowledge the difficulties it poses for all its interpreters. There is much in it that is obscure, and even to pinpoint its central thrust and main message is not easy. The great Martin Luther was right when he said: 'Every man holds that this text is one of the most obscure in the Old Testament' (quoted by H.C. Leupold, *Genesis*, Baker Book House, 1964, vol.2, p.875). 'To study the commentators on the passage', says a recent writer, 'is to realize that an exposition which would satisfy every one in all its details would be so immense a difficulty as to be quite impossible.'

No commentator seems to have satisfactorily resolved all the difficulties. Nevertheless, it is a passage which over very many years has greatly helped me. This is one reason why, before looking at the details, we shall go back into Jacob's past and allow some of the highlights of his earlier experiences to shed their light on this encounter and on God's purposes in his dealings with Jacob here. Also, lest we discourage ourselves before we even begin properly, let us understand that it is possible in looking at this portion of God's Word, to over-emphasize its problems. Those difficulties, and the hazards they contain for every preacher, are more than offset by the rich rewards it holds out to a simple, believing, straightforward study of its main outlines.

One thrust of the entire experience was certainly concerned with the lessons that God wanted to teach Jacob before his entry to the Promised Land. He was the heir of the covenant and its rich spiritual promises. The land was to be his, and his seed's after him. However, the land bordered with that of his brother Esau. This meant that all that was wrong between the two required to be put right. God will not prosper and bless his people if they are living at odds with others and allowing enmity and bad feeling to rule their hearts and their actions. Before matters could be set right, Jacob had to see how wrong he had been in the past. He had to learn new lessons about repentance and humility. He had to learn that being a man of God involves dealing honourably with others. Peniel was important for that reason.

Another purpose that we can see in this encounter concerns Jacob's relationship with God. He has lessons to learn about obedience, about trust, about holiness of heart and meekness of life. He has to learn about walking more closely with God. To put it in the language of the New Testament, he has more to learn about walking 'in the light, as he is in the light' (1 John 1:7). He is in fact never to be quite the same man after this meeting. This is a fundamental principle in the Bible's teaching about the way God deals with his children. It is taught again and again. Every time God lays hold of his people, and manifests his power in them, there is change for good, there is growth in grace, and there is advance in true godliness.

A PHYSICAL ENCOUNTER

There is no doubt that this is a tangible, bodily encounter that confronts us here at Peniel. Far too many commentators reveal their dislike of the supernatural by attempting to explain this incident in terms of dream, or vision, or symbol.

But the closing verse prevents all who accept the authenticity of Scripture from interpreting this in any way other than the actual and literal: 'The children of Israel eat not of the sinew which shrank . . . because he touched the hollow of Jacob's thigh in the sinew that shrank' (v. 32). Also, it is only in this way that we can understand what is meant when we are told that as Jacob left the scene of combat he 'halted upon his thigh' (v.31).

Those facts compel us to regard this as a true, physical experience in the life of Jacob, albeit one that had a deep, spiritual dimension. Everyone who comes to know God's grace in Jesus Christ does have a spiritual experience and, of course, that takes place in time and space and history. We can never ultimately divorce the physical from the spiritual. Man himself lives in both realms. The Bible teaches us that we are soul as well as body. Every approach to this passage which treats it as unhistorical, or as dream, or allegory, or legend is really a huge insult and rebuke to the inspired word of Hosea (12:2-4) who certainly treats it as a historical event, and as a mountain-peak experience in the faith-life of Jacob and God's dealings with him.

A PRAYERFUL ENCOUNTER

It is clear, too, that the encounter involved Jacob in deep and earnest prayer. The inspired comment about this aspect of Peniel which we find in the prophecy of Hosea puts this beyond all doubt, and indicates that prayer must be central in our interpretation of the entire incident. In Hosea we read, 'The LORD hath also a controversy (a word which is important for our understanding of God's dealings with Jacob) with Judah, and will punish Jacob according to his ways; according to his doings will he recompense him. He took his brother by the heel in the womb, and by his strength he had power with (struggled with) God: yea, he had power over the

18

angel, and prevailed: he wept, and made supplication unto him.' This scripture, in turn, seems to be in the mind of the writer to the Hebrews when he writes of Christ's experience in the garden of Gethsemane: 'Who in the days of his flesh, when he had offered up prayers and supplications with strong crying and tears unto him that was able to save him from death, and was heard in that he feared' (Hebrews 5:7).

When we study the Peniel encounter from this point of view it is a powerful reminder that prayer is a very serious and solemn matter indeed. It places us directly and immediately into the hands of God. Perhaps Jacob had never prayed in this fashion before. The terms used to describe the prayer indicate a struggle of the entire man, body and soul, as they do in the case of the Lord Jesus in Gethsemane. The struggle was not imaginary; it was not a vision, nor was it purely spiritual. Hosea's use of it puts it into the realm of practical experience. Jacob seems to have sensed from early on in the contest that his opponent was none other than the Angel of the covenant. He certainly knew it before the Angel had finally departed. His cry, 'I will not let thee go, except thou bless me', is eloquent proof of this for, as Calvin comments, 'The inferior is blessed by the greater' (John Calvin, *Genesis*, Banner of Truth, vol. 2, p.199).

The divine person who is involved in this prayer experience of Jacob is, therefore, the very one who is at the centre of all true prayer, Christ the Mediator and Angel of God's saving covenant. So we learn from the biblical comment of Hosea not only that prayer is a key factor in the wrestling of Jacob, but also that he is being dealt with by the only one through whom God deals with sinful men, the Lord Jesus Christ. The words of Hosea are worth pondering very carefully, for they give us the true focus of Jacob's experience: 'Yea, he had power over the angel, and prevailed: he wept, and made supplication unto him.' The 'man' who wrestled with him is described as an 'angel'. When we compare that with Jacob's own words, 'I have seen God face to face, and my life (soul) is preserved', then we can have no doubt that this is a theophany, that is, a pre-incarnation appearance of Christ in human form (cf. Genesis 12:7; 18:1-15).

We notice too, how Hosea, by way of commentary, tells us that the wrestling was more than a mere physical encounter. It was as the hand-to-hand struggle developed that Jacob sobbed through his entreaty. That is certainly a description of agonizing prayer. Hosea mentions something else that is eloquent of the energy and force with which Jacob sought the blessing. There was a tendency in Jacob not to do anything by halves and it had been displayed even before birth: 'He took his brother by the heel in the womb, and by his strength he had power with God'. That aspect of the character of Jacob is held up to his descendants of a later day by this prophet, so that they might emulate it. All those factors mentioned by Hosea entitle us to look for lessons about earnest, prevailing, wrestling prayer in this encounter at Peniel.

A CRITICAL ENCOUNTER

Jacob! Here is a man whose life reveals what sin has done in human nature, and reveals too what God can do to alter sinful human nature. For the God of all grace has been pleased to use the name of Jacob in one of the covenant titles by which he has identified himself among the children of men. He is the 'God of Jacob', and the one who is the God of a man like Jacob can be our God also. Not only has God revealed himself under this man's name but he has taken the name of Jacob and used it as a title for his beloved people. Down through the ages of the Old Testament era, God's covenant people, the people that he loved with an everlasting love, were known, not as 'Israel' alone, but in times and terms of especial tenderness and grace, as 'Jacob' also. 'He hath not beheld iniquity in Jacob' (Numbers 23:21), and that because of his own gracious, saving work in them and with them.

20

The God of Jacob! He is the God of Jacob because he met with Jacob and blessed him, and we can trace the various dealings of God that led up to this particular time and place in the life and the experience of Jacob. This was an experience that centred in meeting with God, and it was an experience that touched and transformed the man. It was not his conversion experience, but it was the power of the same grace which had converted him, working in his life in a fresh way. God does not leave us when we are converted. He does not convert us and quicken us by the Holy Spirit and then abandon us to ourselves. He continues the work which he inaugurates at conversion. 'He which hath begun a good work in you will perform it until the day of Jesus Christ' (Philippians 1:6).

The sanctifying work of God in the soul of man is a process. It is not, as justification is, a once-for-all act. You are justified the moment you are united to Christ by faith. In that instant your standing before God is made right and it is made right for eternity. At the same time God begins to do something else. He begins to give you a nature that corresponds with your standing. This is the process of sanctification, and it is a process that can have within it at times crisis experiences.

In evangelical circles men have sometimes preached what is known as a theology of 'crisis' sanctification, that is, that there is a second experience which is in its own way just as important as conversion because without it, although you are a Christian, you are not holy. This 'second blessing' type of teaching has led on sometimes to a doctrine of sinless perfection in this life, which is totally unscriptural. The reason men have preached this is because, in the process of sanctification, God has come with amazing, cleansing, transforming experiences which seem to deal with sin 'once and for all'. Then preachers have done something they should never do. They have formed a theology out of their experiences instead of drawing it from the Word of God, and have preached that sanctification consists of a crisis, rather than a process.

Let us be clear in our understanding of the point at issue in this whole matter. Sanctification can have crisis moments when we are brought forward in one bound to walk with God more closely, but nevertheless sin remains in us and God has to deal with it progressively. Jacob knew a crisis experience at Peniel. However the fact is that there was still sin and fault and failure in him after this. Yet his life was never the same again, never as sinfully self-centred as it had been earlier.

An encounter with God! We preach the gospel because we know that such an encounter is a reality. If I did not know that, did not only believe it but know it from my own experience, I would never go into a pulpit to preach again. Do you know anything about it — meeting with God, and knowing God meeting with you? This is the question which will press itself upon our hearts, demanding an answer as we go on to examine the story in greater detail. Before we do that however, we must set the incident against the earlier background. We need to know the kind of man Jacob was and the sort of circumstances that prevailed when he had this amazing experience of God. What were the steps that brought him to Peniel?

2

'And he dreamed, and behold a ladder set up
on the earth, and the top of it reached to heaven:
and behold the angels of God ascending
and descending on it'
(Genesis 28:12).

The theme which occupies us centres on one of the great realities of human experience — that of man in encounter with God. That issues in his coming to know God in his covenant grace and covenant mercy. Put another way, it is coming to know him as the God who has provided a great, all-sufficient, and all-powerful Saviour in Christ his own Son; coming to know him as the God who pardons sinners, and brings them into his own family by the Spirit of adoption.

At the very beginning of man's need as a sinner God made a promise, or perhaps more accurately, unveiled the already settled covenant purpose. This was that he was going to provide a man who would undo the evil of sin and save a people to his own divine glory. That promise is found in Genesis 3:15, where God said to the serpent — who had tempted man into sin — 'And I will put enmity between thee and the woman, and between thy seed and her seed; it shall bruise thy head, and thou shalt bruise his heel.' It was through faith in the promised one who was held out in this covenant, with its subsequent republications to Noah, Abraham, and others, that God graciously revealed himself to men in Old Testament times. Thus he encouraged them to look forward to Messiah — the Anointed One — through whom they could come to know God and be at peace with him.

This is the background against which we must set the account of Jacob at Peniel. God's grace and God's mercy, covenanted and guaranteed to his people through Christ, are illustrated and epitomized for us in the life of Jacob. His experience of God and God's sovereign love through the coming Messiah illustrates for us principles upon which God still deals with sinful, fallen men. His story is a lasting reminder to every generation that encounter with God is the basis of all true godliness. That saving encounter is always in and through the Lord Jesus Christ who, in the fulness of time, came into the world to accomplish the purposes of God's gracious promises.

The text of Scripture which heads the chapter encapsulates the experience of Jacob where, for the first time, we see him come very definitely under the saving influence and grace of God at Bethel. As we probe this Bethel experience, we shall do so under three headings: The Earthly Vessel; The Extraordinary Vision; The Eternal Verities. Using those divisions of thought to mark out our journey and chart our progress let us look first of all at:

THE EARTHLY VESSEL

Here we are looking at the narrative from a very human standpoint, that of Jacob himself. As we apply its lasting principles to our own lives and our experience of God, we will allow the light of New Testament revelation to shine back upon it. In doing this we are confronted with three very simple but basic truths about Jacob, and indeed, about life; he is involved in a journey, a vision, and an awakening. Dwelling on each in turn, let us begin with the fact of:

A lonely journey

Jacob is not a young man now. He is nearer seventy than forty. But he has lived in such a way that he has had to leave home and is in fear of his life at the hand of his own brother. He has twice cheated Esau, first of all of the birthright, then of the covenant blessing of the old, blind father Isaac. The birthright, involving all the prerogatives and inheritance rights that went with being the eldest son, had been signed over to Jacob because of Esau's lust and greed. Although Jacob used guile to persuade Esau to do this, we should remember that Esau himself has the greater fault. His eye and his mind and his heart are all set on earthly things and on how much he can acquire in this life. God, and covenant, and blessing, and eternity are not major considerations with Esau, except for the occasional twinge of conscience and the spasmodic ache of the heart.

There is a great difference between these twin brothers, but we will not stay to examine that just now. It is enough for us to remind ourselves in passing, that the New Testament has painted the character of Esau in chilling words, 'a profane person'. That does not, of course, excuse Jacob nor correct the wrongs that he inflicted on Esau, but he never seems to have flouted God and the things of the Spirit in the same way that Esau did. He did cheat Esau of the birthright and the father's blessing, a blessing calculated to pass on the covenant promise and covenant inheritance that God had given to Abraham. This, and perhaps more especially the promise of land and of plenty which it carried with it, would have been very attractive to Esau. He was so bitter and furious at losing all the material value and prosperity involved in this aspect of the blessing that he was ready to slay his brother.

These are the circumstances, recorded in Genesis 25 and 27, that have sent Jacob out from home on this lonely journey into a strange land. The fact is that God had purposed that both birthright and blessing should go to Jacob, and he and his mother should both have been content to wait God's time to fulfil this aspect of his purpose for Jacob. It was an element in God's plan of which they were certainly aware. It would seem, however, that Isaac had grown forgetful of this

25

fact and wished that the blessing and its fulness might yet go to earthy Esau. This seems to be what provoked Rebekah and Jacob to take things into their own hands. Self-effort and self-reliance, rather than patient waiting for God's time and God's way, characterized their activity. For all their energy, at least on the face of things, everything had gone terribly wrong. For Jacob to remain in the land of covenant promise now was certain death. The only remedy was flight to find refuge with Laban for 'a few days' until Esau settled down (27:43-45), a period which, in fact, would stretch out to twenty years.

In a spiritual sense, this journey is one that every person takes to a greater or lesser extent. We set out, sometimes, into new and strange territory, in attempts to escape from our sin and our wrongdoing, seeking for peace and for refuge, regretting the past and fearing the future. The journey often starts, as this one, in our seeking to handle spiritual responsibilities in worldly ways and in dealing with God along the lines of deception. To try and live by deception is to walk along the narrow line between blessing and cursing. That was the conclusion that must have been forcing itself home to the heart of Jacob in this journey.

It is just here, at this level of Jacob's personal experience, that the story involves not only a journey but something very remarkable which has always arrested attention and made Bethel the focus of much interest for all Bible readers. We are taken into the very heart of the Bethel experience as we look at how Jacob was given:

A disturbed night

The journey merges into vision in an almost casual way. Night begins to fall. The time comes to halt and get some sleep. Whatever the feeling of the heart, or the despair of the mind, there are always the ordinary, ongoing events of our passing days to attend to. So in this case. We read that 'he lighted upon a certain place' (v.11), and because the sun had gone down he prepared to spend the night there. It was not the most congenial place and it was not specially chosen. Circumstances rather than choice dictated the location; a lonely, rugged hillside near the crumbling ruins of an old city. It was probably not very attractive to him as he made his few preparations for the night, yet, it was to be a place that would live in his mind and heart for the rest of his days.

So to the central feature of the experience that awaited Jacob at Bethel. The facts are simple and straightforward. He has a dream, but a dream of a very special kind. The dream is so surprising in its nature and content that the unexpectedness of it never leaves Jacob. It comes out in the language in which the story is given. 'And he dreamed, and behold a ladder . . . and behold the angels of God ascending and descending . . . And, behold, the LORD stood above it' (vv. 12, 13). The wonder of it grips every reader of the story still; we feel the sense of awe that is packed into the repeated 'behold'.

For most of us the story is so familiar that we do not, at first, notice the strangeness of the language. If we were making this story up by the power of our own invention we would do what the story definitely does not do. We would make the angels come down before they mounted up again. We would reverse the order. Did Jacob get it wrong, then? By no means. The way Jesus used the story and the truths about himself which it taught, largely turns upon the order of ascent and descent exactly as we have it here. We will return to it later. What must be stressed at this point is that this abnormal order is preserved and emphasized in John 1:51.

It must have been this very reversal of expected order which first of all brought the message of God and his grace home to Jacob. That message was a revelation of the finest kind to the man in his hour of need. The message brought home the truth that all the time that he had been planning, and scheming, and deceiving, the angels of God had been around him, protecting, leading, ministering to him even though it had all been in the crooked ways of his own cunning and craftiness. They had surrounded him even as he fled from home and was journeying into a strange land, and they had not remained on high after climbing with their news of him, but had come down again to company with him in his onward way.

This is not all. The Lord speaks to him from the top of the ladder, and what marvellous words Jacob hears. They pierce his heart, they shine into his mind, they change all his thought, and they transform him from the inside out, the way the grace of God always does. 'I am the LORD God of Abraham thy father, and the God of Isaac: the land whereon thou liest, to thee will I give it, and to thy seed . . .' On go the familiar, solemn, gracious words of the covenant God which Jacob had so often heard from his father (v.13). It is incredible that it should be happening to him at all, but that it should be happening under his present circumstances — that bows his mind and humbles his heart. The graciousness, the unexpectedness, the wonder of it all make it a marvellous, lasting, and extravagant experience of God for this man. Indeed, those features are the very hallmark of every sinner's experience of God's saving grace.

We need to note carefully exactly what was happening here. God was reaching down to him in the person of the 'Messenger' or 'Angel' as Jacob is to put it on his deathbed many years later (48:16). The Lord was telling him that he stood in the line of covenant blessing and promise, and in precisely the same relationship as had faithful Abraham and gentle Isaac. He was there as the God who brings grace to his people, not on the grounds of their goodness, or their merit, or their worth but on the grounds of his own amazing purposes of saving love and mercy.

The third truth about Jacob's experience is no less important. There was a lonely journey, a disturbed night, and now there is also:

A realistic awakening

It is always the morning hour that tests the value and reality of our dreams. Is it not the case that when we wake up to another day, the dreams and visions and the mystic moments — yes, and even the pledges and promises and the strong resolutions of the night hours — tend to be seen from another perspective? Sometimes the sheer sanity of the waking hour is a great comfort to us after the alarm of our dreams. At other times, it is the cold cynicism of the new day that banishes the mystery of night from our minds and from our hearts. It is then that we can be all too ready to bid the angels leave us. As all of us must, Jacob came to the morning hour. There was no longer any ladder. The angels could not be seen now. The voice of the Eternal was no longer sounding.

Nevertheless, in this instance, the vision of the night stands the test of the morning. The awe of God remained on his spirit. 'This is a terrifying place, the very house of God (Beth-el).' It is clearly stated that he 'was afraid', a term which is used frequently in Scripture, of course, and describes a mixture of terror and adoration. It is an experience that bends men down in worship and reverence and which is very humbling. The place was heavy with the sense of God's holiness and this wrings from his soul a beautiful, meaningful phrase, 'the house of God'. Is it not wonderful, and highly significant, that when this honourable term first surfaces in Scripture it has no reference to temple or synagogue or building at all? The house of God. Where is it? Exactly where you are when you pause to worship, or to pray, or to lift your soul to God in love. What makes any place the house of God, or the doorstep of heaven? The presence of God! You know that too. You know it sometimes when you are alone, in your room, or when, out in the open, the whole world around you is filled with a sense of a presence. Such moments, when they come to us in the immeasurable mercy of God are unforgettable.

I knew that experience when I was shepherding as a young man in my native Argyllshire. High in the hills in the early morning, looking out over a breath-taking scene — the Inner Hebrides, beautiful little islands, studding the blue of the Atlantic ocean — I marvelled at the harmony and balance of what God had made, sometimes feeling terribly alone in it; and then, in the awe of that loneliness, becoming aware of a presence that made the air around me feel thick, and heavy, and still. If you are a Christian you have felt it sometimes, also, in some of the high moments of your life. God makes himself known to his people. He comes to us at unexpected times, in unexpected ways.

Many commentators believe that by using this phrase, Jacob designated the place as a shrine, and that the surrounding peoples would be aware of this fact from the anointed pillar he left behind. Be that as it may, there can be no doubt that for Jacob himself this was to remain a hallowed spot. In truth, every Christian has some such spot to which he can look back and say, 'It was the house of God for me, the very gate of heaven.' The place where grace claimed the soul, and life bowed to the lordship of Jesus must always be a hallowed spot for the believer. The house of God for his people in every age is just the place where God makes himself known, where he comes to them with his tender mercy and his loving-kindness, where he visits them with his salvation. At Bethel Jacob made vows to God, not in any sense in the way of bargaining, but as whole-hearted response to the revelation of grace and love.

In the next place we must give attention to:

THE EXTRAORDINARY VISION

Prelude to the dream

For Jacob the sheepman, sleeping rough is nothing new. He chooses a stone for his pillow, and wrapped in his rough shepherd's cloak falls asleep. There he is, a sleeping man. But to the eye of heaven he is far more than that. He is a man with a past, a present, and a future. His past has been filled with guile, stained with guilt, marked with sinful, selfish ambition. Not too pleasant a past; yet, one shared in a sense by all of us.

He is also a man with a present. It holds many fears. It has emerged from and has been shaped by the past. That is what most heavily weights it all for Jacob as the night is closing swiftly in on him. His present carries great loneliness. It cuts him off from all that is good and precious and warm and lovely in his past, and closes him into fears and forebodings which, surely, he had never experienced in his life before. In the midst of his uneasy present he sleeps eventually, knowing only that troubled sleep in which there is little peace for the restless heart. He finds no release from the painful consciousness, the ache of being exiled by reason of his own deceit. Even so, as he drifts into his fitful sleep he is probably glad to be in the solitude, because of his sin.

He is a man with a future. What will it hold? In all probability he had asked himself that question many times in the two or three days of his flight. Nothing was sure. Nothing was definite for him. He was going to the land of Laban. Would Laban receive him? He could not know those things in the present and so they left the future hazy, uncertain, and over it all so many question marks. He was turning his back upon all the certainties he had enjoyed in his life up until that time. Would he ever come back? He knew he had sinned. The fact was in the forefront of thought all the time. Would the God of his father Abraham and his father Isaac now cast him off for ever? Would the cold mass that filled his breast and made him feel so miserable ever really go away? Would he never come to know the living God? Would he have to live and die under his curse, because he had sought the covenant blessing in the wrong way? Had he, perhaps, committed the unpardonable sin?

31

This is all that this man had as he lay down on his hard pillow that night. A past of deceitfulness and sin, a present of loneliness and fear, a future of uncertainty and doubt. It is easy for most of us to put ourselves into Jacob's position that night. Perhaps you are in it yourself. It is an unpleasant one, but all too common. It is part of the heritage of our fallen nature and a continual reminder of the power of sin over our lives.

Illumination on the dream

It will help us greatly if we take a wider biblical perspective on what was really happening at Bethel. We have the advantage of being able to do this by way of a rather unusual, and at first sight somewhat oblique, reference of the Lord Jesus to this incident. In this reference, rays of New Testament light which shine back into the story illumine it for us, and help us interpret it in relation to the purposes of God. In Jacob's time these were being gradually unfolded, but were not to find final manifestation until they were seen in Jesus Christ himself.

Although their ultimate disclosure lay far ahead in the future as Jacob lay down at Bethel, those purposes undergird and determine all that God is doing with him. Of course, we can understand them in a way which Jacob himself could not. What we must avoid doing, therefore, is to read our understanding into the personal feelings and experience of Jacob. We must reckon with the fact that it is not possible to know precisely how clearly Jacob was able to interpret all that happened, but we can be quite certain he knew it was the dealing of grace. Whatever his own theological appreciation of the encounter, we do know that it elicited his faith, and brought a new, personal trust to life which made him conscious of the care and goodness of God.

It is in John 1:47-51 that we find Jesus making reference to the episode at Bethel. He is dealing with Nathanael, calling him into open discipleship. When he sees him Jesus says,

'Behold an Israelite indeed, in whom is no guile!' Here is a man, Jesus is saying, in whom there is no 'Jacob'. He is an 'Israel', one who has striven with God, one over whom, and in whom, God has revealed his power. His statement almost stuns Nathanael who responds, 'Whence knowest thou me?' 'Before that Philip called thee, when thou wast under the fig tree, I saw thee', comes the rejoinder. That drew an immediate, and at first sight surprising, confession from Nathanael. 'Rabbi,' he said, 'thou art the Son of God; thou art the King of Israel.' Why was Nathanael so surprised? Why did this remark convince him that here was one to whom belonged the absolute titles of Messiah?

It is highly likely that Nathanael had been meditating under his shady fig tree — many Jewish homes had them for this very purpose — during the siesta hour of the day. A pious, godly man, he was not asleep but was spending his spare time in contemplation, reflecting on the things of God. It is also very probable that his thoughts were dwelling on this remarkable incident of the patriarch Jacob at Bethel, and that he was thinking of the vision of the ladder and the angels. This appears from the way Jesus responded to the sudden, believing confession that his words had drawn from Nathanael. 'Because I said unto thee, I saw thee under the fig tree, believest thou? thou shalt see greater things than these . . . hereafter ye shall see heaven open, and the angels of God ascending and descending upon the Son of Man.' All this alerts us to the lasting spiritual realities of Bethel and to the theological significance of the story.

Postscript to the dream

Bethel transformed a worldly man into a worshipper. Before this, Jacob appears to us as a runaway from the results of his sin, a troubled man in search of himself and of the divine purpose for his life, forcing the pace in that search, and then knowing that instead of obtaining peace he had merely aggravated his own guilt. A lonely fugitive when he flung himself down for sleep on the second or third night of his trek, and more than 150 miles from his home in Beersheba, the bleak, rocky surroundings at the ancient town of Luz must have reflected his own gloomy, inward condition.

After this night and its encounter, however, there is a complete change in Jacob. From this point onwards he is a partner with God. He has been given, and is trusting in, God's covenant promises. He knows what it is to wonder and worship and he knows that God is not far away but in fact is very near. In a very real sense, the world has become a different place for Jacob. God is interested in it, and God's power and glory and promises and purpose are concerned with it, and have all to be reckoned with. All that makes Jacob a very different man from the guilty fugitive who had lain down with the coming of night. Such encounter, with the changes it brings, has been repeated again and again through the history of God's dealings with his people. The intrusion of grace always transforms the course of a person's life.

Here is the central and important part of this vision of the night. God has spoken and has made himself known to Jacob. When the voice of the Eternal comes, it is not, after all, the voice of destruction that inward fear had anticipated, but the voice of tender renewal and promise. Later, in Genesis 48:3, Jacob directly identifies the Angel of the Lord with God Almighty (*El Shaddai*), and tells us that it was this one who had blessed him at Bethel. Thus, we have here a manifestation of the Son of God himself; the first appearance, but not the last, which Jacob was to experience.

Without dwelling on the importance of this revelation to Jacob, we observe the following. Not only did he stand in need of repentance and forgiveness for the present but, as we have seen, in need of assurance for the future. It is only grace which can meet all those needs for any one of us. The promise concludes with the undertaking that God will restore Jacob to the land, pledging therefore all the help, protection, guidance, and blessing that Jacob will need. How wonderfully all the questions of his heart have been answered as the ancient covenant promise is sealed to him now by the mouth of the Lord himself. 'Behold, I am with thee, and will keep thee in all places whither thou goest, and will bring thee again into this land; for I will not leave thee, until I have done that which I have spoken to thee of' (v. 15).

It is worth pointing out that the statement 'I will not leave thee, until I have done . . .' does not imply that once God has fulfilled his promise he will abandon Jacob — God does not work in that way. Instead, the statement contemplates all the hazards likely to occur between the present assertion and that remoter, historical point of its fulfilment. God is giving Jacob the assurance that the promises then given to him will most certainly be fulfilled. This pledge of God's presence with him is the final guarantee that the promise must be brought to its full realization. From the lips of our great Redeemer himself, every Christian believer has precisely the same assurance, 'Lo, I am with you alway, even unto the end of the world' (Matthew 28:20).

The final point to notice about this vision and its revelation is simply this. Until now Jacob had known only about God. From now on he knows him in a different way. He knows him in an intimate, personal way, and on the grounds of God's own promise can claim him for evermore as his own God. Before he had known of the Lord only as the God of Abraham and the God of Isaac. From this moment on, he is to know him, and think of him, trust him and pray to him as his own God also. The gracious things he had heard from childhood had now become real in his own experience.

We must proceed to the third and final division of our study. Here we look especially at the theological and doctrinal truths which it is fitted to impress upon us, and the lessons we can learn for our own Christian lives. So we look at:

THE ETERNAL VERITIES

We are looking at the background to Peniel and Jacob's experience there. That experience has as its central feature the reality of encounter with God. In a sense, this lies at the very heart of the gospel of God's grace, in all its teachings right through the Scriptures of truth. It is God bringing his own, loved, elect people into a living relationship with himself in Christ, and by faith in Christ. This must be much in our minds as we go on to look at some abiding principles in God's dealings with us, as they are illustrated here at Bethel, and interpreted in the light that the New Testament casts back on Bethel. Our thoughts will move once more along three lines of exploration here.

The link between earth and heaven

The sole function of a ladder is to enable one to climb up or down, to reach what is above or what is below. The one Jacob saw in his dream was firmly set on earth. That has to be emphasized. The foot of it seems to have been near to Jacob and the top of it reached all the way to heaven. That is unusual. Nothing on earth reaches all the way to heaven. Jacob is being told there is a link between earth and heaven. The two are not so remote and so separate that they never can, and never will, meet. There is communication between heaven and earth, between God and man. That was an important truth for Jacob to learn. Indeed, it is an important truth for all men to learn.

A recent study on Jacob at Bethel expresses this thought well. It emphasizes that Jacob 'sees another realm — a kingdom! — besides the one in which he has travelled and eaten and slept. He sees creatures and powers that belong to the other realm rather than to this. He sees in it the place of God himself, the ruler and creator of this world. He sees that there is a way or a ladder from one world to another, and traffic going on between' (Ronald S. Wallace, *Isaac and Jacob*, SPCK, 1982, p.81).

36

Attention has already been drawn to the order of movement on the ladder as being the very opposite of what we should expect. Surely, we think, any correspondence with heaven must come down first, and only then go upwards in return. Even so, this is the order that Jesus mentions to Nathanael also — ascending and descending. Significantly, Jesus relates that ladder to himself and to the work which he had come to accomplish. Looking ahead to all he had to do by way of atonement and reconciliation, in death and resurrection, he said, 'Ye shall see heaven open, and the angels of God ascending and descending upon the Son of Man' (John 1:51).

The interpretation of the ladder

In identifying himself with the ladder Jesus proclaims the essential message of Jacob's dream. He himself as Son of Man — giving himself the title which underlines his human nature and his saving work as man — is to be the one link of communication between earth and heaven. He is that 'new and living way' spoken of in the Epistle to the Hebrews (10:20). 'No man', he taught the world, 'cometh unto the Father, but by me' (John 14:6). Interestingly, he so turns around the expression of Nathanael's faith as to lay the stress on his earthly work and his human nature. Nathanael had confessed him as 'Son of God . . . King of Israel', and so he was. He was also Son of Man and it was in this capacity that the King of Israel was to suffer and be crucified and to bear our sins in his own body.

Only the incarnate Son could suffer. Only the incarnate Son could die and pay the price of sin and of guilt. Only in this office, as the High Priest of God 'taken from among men', could the way to the Father — closed by sin — be reopened. Only thus could communication with heaven be re-established. It was in the efficacy of his atoning work, accomplished on earth, that 'he entered in once into the holy place, having obtained eternal redemption . . . into heaven itself, now to appear in the presence of God for us' (Hebrews 9:12,24). It is in the Son that the Father has all his dealings with the children of men. There is no other pathway of communication. The Bible puts it starkly but clearly; 'Neither is there salvation in any other: for there is none other name under heaven given among men, whereby we must be saved' (Acts 4:12).

The word 'angel' means 'messenger', and so the sight of the angels on the ladder introduces the idea of message or report. What message went up from the suffering and death of the Son of Man? The 'odour of a sweet smell, a sacrifice acceptable, wellpleasing to God' (Philippians 4:18). The death of Christ involves blood-shedding, a solemnity which lies at the very heart of what sacrifice means. We have it in such biblical phrases as 'the blood of the covenant', and the New Testament speaks of 'the blood of sprinkling, that speaketh better things than that of Abel' (Hebrews 12:24). What was the cry of the blood of Abel which ascended from earth to heaven? It was the cry for vengeance. The cry of the blood of Christ is altogether different. It calls for reconciliation, and peace, and forgiveness of the sins of all his people. What a message! What a Messenger! What a marvellous communication as it reaches all the way from the cross on earth, to the throne in heaven!

The way of continual access

Although Jacob did not see all those matters as clearly as we can in the light of Christ's finished work, he did have faith to rest in God. That is certain. Like ourselves if we are Christians he is a 'son of Abraham' in the spiritual sense and, like Abraham, he is reckoned as righteous on account of faith. Perhaps, again like Abraham, he saw Christ's day from afar 'and was glad'. However that may be, it is clear that God was graciously and tenderly imposing his covenant terms upon

Jacob, and giving his blessing with his eye upon the finished work of the Mediator who was yet to come, and who was yet to seal all those promises with his precious blood. Can we doubt that, in some measure at least, Jacob's faith was directing itself also to the 'seed' who had been dimly revealed in the promises to his forebears as the coming one who was the medium and channel of God's blessings?

The outstanding truth emerging from this brief account we have of Jacob's experience at Bethel is this. It informs us how God suddenly and unexpectedly broke into the life of this 'supplanter', this 'deceiver' who was fleeing for his very life, and unveiled the covenantal purpose which concerned him, sealed the covenantal promises to him, and assured him of God's covenantal presence with him. In doing that God conveyed to Jacob the essential elements which are the core and life of saving, Christian experience still. What claims the soul for the worship of God is the actual revelation to us of mercy, grace, and the Lord's presence with us in the way. Those who come to see and accept God's gracious provision and God's protective presence are those whose lives are constrained into worship — not just in the services and meetings of the church, but in every moment of life. The whole world becomes a 'Beth-el' for them, and the greatest of realities is the reality of God.

Jacob's response at Bethel is indicative of the impression the entire experience had made on his heart. He 'rose up early in the morning, and took the stone that he had put for his pillows, and set it up for a pillar, and poured oil upon the top of it'. Jacob took his pillow and transformed it into an altar and pillar of lasting remembrance. There he worshipped God, making solemn vows of service, obedience, and tithes. Those are significant actions and they speak clearly of the kind of man Jacob had become through the great revelation he had been given.

Commitment and consecration are the invariable responses

to a true work of God's grace in the heart of a sinner. Those are the things which characterize Jacob as he takes leave of Bethel. He is not yet perfect — neither are we — but he is walking in the light that he has, the light that the Lord God has given him. That is much. Indeed, in a very real sense, that is everything.

When we take Bethel and set it into the framework of the New Testament gospel, it rings wonderfully true to Christian experience. Of course there is a difference. The difference favours us, and demands more of us than was required of Jacob. When we apply to our own situation the principles taught Jacob at Bethel, how much clearer our light than his. How much more we have, how much more we should give, how much more God has a right to demand of us. He came near to Jacob in the Angel of the covenant. In the same one he has brought us near to himself. Paul puts it emphatically, memorably, 'But now in Christ Jesus ye who sometimes were far off are made nigh by the blood of Christ' (Ephesians 2:13).

For us in the gospel age, that provides the ultimate revelation of God and his grace. From earth to heaven the final cry of redemption's agony has gone up and been heard — 'My God, my God, why hast thou forsaken me?' (Matthew 27:46). So also has the final cry of redemption's triumph, 'It is finished' (John 19:30). By the Holy Spirit the Lord Jesus Christ is still the one medium of communication between earth and heaven. From heaven's throne messages of assurance and peace come down to us. The cries of penitent sinners, the prayers of the people of God, the unexpressed desires of the longing soul, all ascend and are heard because of Christ's atoning death. The responses of grace and of mercy, the purchased blessings of God for his children, are bestowed in answer to the intercession of the exalted Christ, our Priest and Advocate (1 John 2:1). All the benefits of redemption descend upon us by virtue of his mediatorial work, and so are ours through him, and only because of him.

As Hermon's dew, the dew that doth
  on Sion's hill descend:
For there the blessing God commands,
  life that shall never end.
    (Psalm 133:3 Scottish Psalter)

3

'And Jacob was left alone; and there wrestled
a man with him until the breaking of the day'
(Genesis 32:24).

In considering the experience of Jacob at Peniel we are looking at this basic theme of Scripture, that God can be known,
and that God can be encountered in grace and mercy. We
have looked at the subject of Peniel in a general way and mentioned some of the great truths that thread their way through
to us from Jacob's encounter with the Angel of the covenant,
that pre-incarnation visit of Christ to him.

We have also looked at the circumstances behind the story,
at how Jacob had to leave home running for his life, marked
out by his deceitfulness, and apprehensive about what the
future might hold. We looked at that remarkable experience
he had at Bethel and how the God of grace revealed himself to
him and unveiled his covenant. From then on he knows God,
recognizes God's hand in his life, and despite his own self-
reliance and pride and guile, he recognizes himself as being in
the covenant favour of God, as being in the place of God's
blessing. Nothing of that belief is misplaced. It reflects his
standing before God and his place in God's saving plan and
purpose.

Twenty years have passed. Jacob has had hard times — and
prosperous ones — and now he is on the way back to his own
land, the land of promise, the land of which God had spoken
to Abraham and Isaac. It is the land which God had pledged
to give to him as he slept on its borders in his flight out of it.

The twenty years have been full of life and activity and interest. With a sharp, astute mind and sheer hard work he has been making his way well. He has been amassing and accumulating wealth, and wives, and goods. He has lived in association with his uncle Laban — a man who has proved even more calculating than himself, and more miserly than most of those we meet on the pages of Scripture. Because of this, the association has been more of a business arrangement than a family one. Laban used Jacob and Jacob's faith for his own ends and his own enrichment. This was so, despite the conviction that he was being blessed for Jacob's sake.

Jacob now faces the prospect of meeting another enemy — this time one of his own making — Esau. Jacob decided to advise Esau of his imminent return, and 'sent messengers before him to Esau his brother'. They had come back with the terrifying news that Esau was hard on their heels with an army of four hundred men (32:3-6). For those days, that was a very large force of men and indicates that Esau must often have been embroiled in warring with neighbouring peoples. It boded ill for Jacob and his family and flocks. Jacob had left home because his brother threatened his life. Now, recalling Esau's temper and hatred, he must have felt that his little group of people would soon be the subjects of a real bloodbath. These are the immediate circumstances which lead up to Peniel, and past events fill them with the threat of violence and death.

Let us look firstly at:

THE SETTING OF THE ENCOUNTER

'And Jacob was left alone . . .' One of the sad features of modern society and modern life, especially in our great cities, is the sheer inability of many people to 'get away' from others and be with God. Christians need often to give time to being in the presence of God.

Seeking a way of escape

Jacob seeks God because of danger. The danger is largely the result of his own wrongdoing. In fact, what is happening is very plain and very simple. His chickens have come home to roost. His past is marching round on him to confront him once more. As it does so it carries a real threat for his future. What a solemn spiritual reality this is, one with which we are all familiar. Uneasiness and dread are not easily despatched. Our past, which perhaps we had forgotten, begins to trouble the present and menace the future. It is a microscopic picture of all men as they try to escape a sinful past and find that, do what they may, the God of judgement is all the time out there in front of them, a threat to their future peace and their future prospects. 'Be sure your sin will find you out' (Numbers 32:23).

Jacob takes all sorts of precautions. He weighs up his situation very carefully. He examines his options, and he decides which are the easiest for him. He wishes to sort things out so that, whatever happens, he will not have to face Esau. He will face loss in his flocks and herds; he will face loss in his men and his family; he will face even God; the one thing which he just will not do, which he cannot do, is face Esau. Notice the words of verse 20; 'I will appease him with the present that goeth before me, and *afterward I will see his face.*' His sharp mind is considering the alternatives, assessing the chances, seeking an exit.

His shrewd, worldly-wise calculations are reflected in the way he grouped his presents. As matters turn out, his strategies are going to be unnecessary, yet Jacob must go through all these preparations, exerting his talents, making his efforts, achieving his best. It is what we all do when we are really up against things. But God is in control, and Jacob is to be taught lessons in this incident that he will never forget. He resolves to use diplomacy. We should notice the implications of those words in verse 20. Jacob did not really wish to find grace in the eyes of his brother at all, although that was the verbal message he sent — 'that I may find grace in thy sight' (v.5). However, actions speak louder than words.

The huge present that went with his message — 550 animals — said something more than his words implied. Its intimation was that Jacob really wanted to 'buy off' a man he could only regard not as a brother but as an enemy. Also, the animals that he was sending were his as the fruit of God's blessing over the years. What does this indicate? It means, in essence, that Jacob at this point, because of his fear, was ready to relinquish his 'blessing' to Esau. In fact, when he met Esau he actually said to him, 'Take, I pray thee, my blessing . . . because God hath dealt graciously with me, and because I have enough. And he urged him' (33:11). The reference is to this 'gift' of appeasement, all of which he owed purely to the faithfulness of God.

The actual terms in which the message was couched — with his use of 'servant' for himself, and 'lord' for Esau — also attract our attention. They were very wrong. By using such words Jacob put at risk his family leadership. All the rights, privileges, and duties of the birthright were, by implication at least, being handed straight back to Esau, as he bargained with the birthright that had already cost him so dearly. These anxious efforts indicate how deeply his fear of Esau ran. They also reflect how little he trusted God.

Sensing a need of God

We have to take stock of more than guile and self-reliance in Jacob. The story takes us further into the complicated heart of the man, and it also takes us deeply into the gracious dealings of God with him. So, we also take note of his prayer. In fact, it is one of the most beautiful of the brief prayers recorded in Genesis, and worthy of the warmest Christian heart and the strongest Christian faith. Moreover it grows out of a sense of need.

His pleading with God acknowledges covenantal mercies and faithfulness. It also acknowledges the footing on which all that he now owns has come to him — it has all flowed from the free grace, the covenant love of God. 'I am not worthy of the least of all the mercies, and of all the truth (faithfulness), which thou hast shewed unto thy servant; for with my staff I passed over this Jordan; and now I am become two bands' (v. 10). It is all too easy for us to miss the awe which filled Jacob's soul here. The facts are rehearsed by him, and they are more than true. He had crossed this river with nothing but his shepherd's crook. Now he is returning, and in terms of his time and culture he is returning as a very wealthy man indeed.

The heart of his petition, however, is in verse 11, 'Deliver me, I pray thee, from the hand of my brother, from the hand of Esau: for I fear him, lest he will come and smite me.' Jacob is being plain and honest. The verb used — deliver — is on his lips again at the end of the story, after the night of wrestling is over and the true victory, that of the heart and the spirit, has been won. After Jacob has come through to the dawn of a new day, he reflects on the experience of the night and he rightly marvels, 'I have seen God face to face, and my life is preserved (delivered)' (v.30).

He had been preserved, even though he, a sinner, had been tightly in the grip of God. In that greater deliverance there had been the lesser as well. It was only when Jacob was blessed by God (v.29) that he was delivered from Esau, and the dread of Esau. For him, as for all who are so blessed, the words of John hold true — 'Perfect love casteth out fear.' By then he had discovered that seeing the 'face' of God was something even more fearsome than seeing the 'face' of Esau.

Let us look, in the second place, at:

THE SOLITUDE OF THE ENCOUNTER

Here we draw nearer to the heart of our subject, and the verses of the chapter with which we are especially concerned. The introductory phrase, 'Jacob was left alone' (v.24), is an immediate and graphic reminder that there are places and areas in the history of personal, spiritual experiences of God's grace where we have to be brought into solitude. There are, of course, various kinds of solitude. One is solitariness of spirit, a loneliness of the soul, of which we must take account here.

The alienation of sin

The solitary experience of Jacob at this point can largely be traced to sin. Such isolation as he must have felt then is one of the terrible effects of sin. Sin is not just a theory, not just a doctrine; it is a fact. It is a power working in our hearts and in our lives. We know, not only from the Word of God but from our own living, everyday experience, that sin severs relationships.

Sin brings separation into three specific areas of man's life, each in the sphere of fellowship, the area of human experience designed to fulfil and satisfy the deepest demands of his nature and being. They are three areas of relationship intended to enrich and beautify life for the creature whom God had made in his own image. Into those precious places sin has intruded its evil presence, bringing its disruptive power with it and so deepening man's sense of loneliness and alienation. The Bible demonstrates again and again the power of sin to separate in those areas of human life. We may very briefly illustrate this solemn fact.

Sin separates man from God

The Genesis story of Adam and Eve tells us that. The doctrine of the fall of man is true and enters into all our human experience. No sooner had man sinned than sin separated him from the fellowship that he had enjoyed with God. He was alienated from the Creator. There was a departure of the Spirit of God who had indwelt Adam, and he was left in a world which, although stamped with the power of its great Creator, no longer carried for him the sense of God's presence. That consequence prevails in every unrenewed man.

The heart which thinks itself no longer able to believe in God, the sad, uncertain heart of the atheist is the fruit of sin's power to alienate the human spirit from God. In some measure even the Christian has experience of this reality. We know that alienation for ourselves; we have known it all our days — a loneliness of soul because of sin. You know it as a Christian also when you sin deliberately and go against God. When you lose his fellowship and the sense of his presence, you know that alienation has come in and you have been separated from him. This Jacob knew too.

Sin separates man from man

Sin had been separating Jacob from everything that endues life with its best qualities, and it had been happening for many years. Behind this story we read, 'And Isaac sent away Jacob' (Genesis 28:5). Further back we will find, as we have been seeing, a terrible rift, a bitterness, an alienation between himself and his twin brother. His worst enemy in the world is the man who was formed in the same womb at the same time as he himself was given the spark of life. What a sad commentary this is. Their father had prayed for his wife 'because she was barren' and then we are told, 'When her days to be delivered were fulfilled, behold, there were twins in her womb' (25:24). This of course points up the sovereignty and mystery of God's dealings with men, but it also highlights the ominous fact that sin has a fearsome power to separate and alienate even those who are bound in the closest ties of blood and nature.

Alienation finds graphic illustration in Jacob's personal

history at every single turn. Given its focus in his relationship with his twin, it forms the great point of tension in his life, running through his story until Peniel, and being swept away only by the reconciliation with Esau to which Peniel leads. We find this tension at its peak as he leaves his father's home to go to Padan-aram (Genesis 28:5). It epitomizes the alienation we find as a major factor in all his relationships in that country, even with the beloved Rachel. Now it forms the dominant factor in the forlorn situation in which he finds himself.

This severance of man from man had begun as soon as sin entered the world. From the account given us in Genesis 3, we see how quickly and effectively sin separated Adam from Eve. Adam acknowledged that God had given Eve to him, yet he immediately lays all the blame on her: 'The woman whom thou gavest to be with me, she gave me of the tree, and I did eat' (Genesis 3:12). What Adam was now too blind to see was that in making this charge against Eve he was driving a wedge into their fellowship, accusing her, and with every word he said, alienating her — his helpmeet — thus widening the gap that sin had already carved into their relationship.

How often, in myriad ways, is the same awesome, awful truth reflected in human experience still! Look at the broken homes all round our land today, broken homes even in our Christian churches. How does it happen? Why does it happen? It is because of the alienating, sundering power of sin. One of the things the gospel does is to heal first of all the breach between God and the soul. That is wonderful. Then it heals the breach between man and man and it restores us into the peace and beauty of fellowship, the kind of fellowship we know and treasure whenever Christians meet to worship and enjoy God. That is just an illustration of what an astounding effect the gospel produces in its reversals of the working and power of sin in human life.

In every one of us there is a deep divide in terms of personal peace, a division in which the spirit of enmity lives and flourishes — me at enmity with myself. No unregenerate man is ever completely at peace with himself. There is a disorder of a spiritual and psychological kind deep in the heart of fallen man. The healing of that division is one of the great features of spiritual restoration effected when a man finds Christ. To be at peace with God is to be at peace with oneself. That is reflected in the prayer of the psalmist, 'Unite my heart to fear thy name' (Psalm 86:11).

Even when healed in regeneration and union to Christ this inward divide leaves its legacies behind it. There is a lingering sense of alienation that carries on, to some extent at least, into the life of the Christian believer. There is certainly healing and integration of personality in regeneration and conversion, and we must not devalue it in any way, but the process is not complete until we are home in heaven. There is still a battle. There is a new principle which is ruling but there is an old principle which wars with it. Professor John Murray used to speak of it as 'the entail of sin', indwelling sin, and it causes tensions, and inward, spiritual strife even in the Christian believer. The story of Jacob wrestling at Peniel reflects those spiritual realities. Other matters also call for consideration.

The awareness of guilt

Jacob was afraid. Why? Because Esau was coming back. But Esau was his twin brother. He should have been rejoicing and looking forward to seeing Esau after years of separation. Not so. This other factor was at work. Guilt was chilling the heart of this man. He could not escape the thought that he had wronged Esau, and that his present difficulties all traced back to his own sin. It was his guilty conscience which interpreted the purpose of Esau's coming in terms of threat and bloodshed. When we sin against another, or another sins against us, how quick we are to form conclusions! Guilt will not permit anything else. Whatever Esau's intention might be at this stage, Jacob was certain that he was about to be visited with vengeance.

For twenty years he seems to have buried the memory of his sin, as we all do. We put sin behind us, we bury it deep into forgetfulness, and think we are finished with it. Then, suddenly something unexpected happens, memory is awakened, sin is resurrected, and it stares us in the face and we know our guilt once more. There is only one grave from which sin cannot be resurrected, and that is the grave to which the Saviour took it, when he had paid its price upon the cross. Have you believed upon Jesus? Do you know that your sin and guilt are buried? Perhaps it is sin such as you can never forget. Happily, the message of the gospel is that when sin has been forgiven, God forgets it: 'Their sins and their iniquities will I remember no more' (Hebrews 8:12).

The accusations of conscience

God has left a monitor in every human breast. As it was with Herod, so it was with Jacob. Conscience raised the remembrance of guilt, and the whole miserable business was back, filling his mind with bitter thoughts, weighing his heart with leaden feelings, stirring him into anxious activity. We may cover conscience, we may quieten conscience, we may stifle its strident voice. We may do all this and then, all of a sudden, it cries out against us again and is as powerful and alarming as ever. It cannot finally be hushed into silence. It distinguishes between right and wrong; between sin and holiness; between good and evil. It functions like this because, of course, God has written the principles of his law in our hearts. Here, on the borders of the land to which he is returning, memory and conscience are hard at work, the one provoking the other on the side of righteousness and of God.

All this points up the reason why Jacob was 'left alone'. He was far more alone, perhaps, than some of us will ever realize. Only those who have been brought through the experience of facing up to their sin, and its guilt, and its far-reaching consequences, will appreciate how alone Jacob was in this place of his solitude. Perhaps it is since conversion you have felt it as God has been working in you, convincing you again of the power of sin to alienate and separate.

What happens is this. As God touches you through the preaching of the Word, or the reading of it, or through the witness of some godly brother or sister in Christ, you feel the power of guilt being stirred up. You hear the Word being preached, and God begins to put his finger on this and that and the other in your life. Perhaps it is the way you have fallen off from prayer; perhaps neglect of the Word; perhaps the forsaking of family worship in the home with the children. It may even be something far more vile and foul than any of those things; sin which makes you feel unclean among God's people, and which has brought the haunting fear that you are not a Christian at all.

The awesomeness of being alone

Alone with a Sovereign God

Have you ever been left alone with nothing but your sin? That is a desolating experience. Indeed, being alone is itself an awesome thing. It reflects a tremendous truth about the very stuff of human existence, and about how, as his creatures, it is impossible to be completely autonomous, or free of the overriding control of God. This is an aspect of life that few people have the courage to face up to, or to acknowledge. Yet it is a fact of life from which there is no ultimate escape. It is also a fact from which the Christian believer should draw great comfort.

A sense of isolation comes into every area of our life in which the tensions between the rule of God and our own human dependence are felt. That is why we must give special attention for a moment to this formidable matter of the lordship of God over us all. It is sometimes brought home with overwhelming power and makes us feel afraid. It is without doubt one of the surest factors of our existence. If God is truly God then the logical conclusion we come to is that he is in complete and ultimate control of all things, even of the life and destiny of every man, woman, and child. That is the teaching of the Bible, and it is teaching which is verified in all human experience. Above all others, it is the fact which makes us feel how awesome a thing individuality is. The gift of personality, of self-consciousness, of self-awareness — these involve solitude before God, our Creator.

This becomes evident along two or three simple lines of thought. There is, for example, a solitary aspect attaching to our very birth, for we were brought into this world with no say at all in the matter. The sovereign lordship of God marked the beginning of your days, even if you attempt to deny or deride such a thing as the predestination and foreordination of God. You had no say in when you would be born or where, or who your father and mother would be, or what colour your skin should be. Why then, when it comes into the realm of grace and salvation, should you feel at all uneasy when the Bible, or the preacher, begins to talk about the election of grace, or God's predestination, or his foreordering of whatever comes to pass? Those things are so clearly behind the experiences of Jacob, and so closely bound up with his amazing encounter with God at Peniel.

You are alone in birth, you are alone in death, you are alone in all the great crisis experiences of life. Those are experiences which you can share with none other. They draw you off into the sphere of your individuality and shut you in with God. You may be in a crowded church and God begins dealing with you in grace, convicting you of your sin and your need. At such an hour you forget the crowd. How often over the years people who have been dealt with by the Holy Spirit have afterwards come to me and said, 'I felt you were talking just to me; I felt God had singled me out from the crowd, and was speaking very specifically to me.' The Spirit can isolate you in a crowded building with that solitude in which you know yourself alone with God.

There is one particular in which the experience of solitariness is seen in greatest solemnity. There is a sure moment coming for each of us when we shall be very sharply aware of an experience which we can share with no one else. Beyond death, judgement awaits every soul of man. There, we will be completely on our own with God. There, no other can intervene, no other can help, no other can hinder. Just as our birth is peculiarly our own, our sin, our response to the gospel, and our death, so also is our final dealing with God. 'We must all appear before the judgment seat of Christ,' says the apostle Paul; 'that every one may receive the things done in his body, according to that he hath done, whether it be good or bad' (2 Corinthians 5:10). That will be a loneliness all will experience, but none will share.

Alone through saving grace

There is a loneliness other than that caused by sin. There are times and places of solitude full of power and blessing, wrapped around with the fellowship of God.

In a sense, the isolation of grace had been evident in Jacob ever since he was born. Indeed, grace had been operative in him in a mighty, divine, and sovereign way even before his birth. We cannot fail to notice how strongly the lordship of God is affirmed for us in the life of Jacob. Paul illustrates God's sovereignty from the relationship of these two brothers and the attitudes which divide them so sharply. He states the point unambiguously: 'Therefore hath he (God) mercy on whom he will have mercy' (Romans 9:18). This New Testament application of Jacob's story with its focus on the tension between him and Esau highlights the way grace distinguishes the objects of God's saving love. Ultimately, the differences between men are traced back to that fact.

Let me ask a question. Why do you attend Christian conventions? Why do you listen to the Christian gospel or read Christian books, instead of throwing your life and your time away as so many others are doing? Why are you a Christian believer and, perhaps, as in the case of Jacob and Esau, others of your family are sceptical, unconverted, unforgiven? Many Christians look back with awe upon the fact that God has had mercy on them and has passed by more likely looking people. Perhaps you are saying to your heart even now, Why me? The theological perspective of this story of Jacob cannot be left aside. We have the distinguishing, sovereign, electing, covenant love of God, finding perfect illustration in the life of this man. It brings strains and tensions into his experience, but in the midst of them all, this great truth stands out. God's covenant grace has been setting him apart for blessing even from the womb.

There can be no doubt that the isolating process of grace began in the womb — the Scripture is explicit and clear on that point. It is also clear that it was operative then because it had taken its rise in eternity, in the love of the God who purposed to save Jacob, and to save him in a way which would manifest his sovereign glory and grace. Hence, the whole process which unfolds in the life of Jacob is an unveiling of covenant love encompassing even the sinnership of Jacob. Another great theological principle of God's saving grace shines through to us: 'But where sin abounded, grace did much more abound: that as sin hath reigned unto death, even so might grace reign through righteousness unto eternal life by Jesus Christ our Lord' (Romans 5:20,21).

It was Jacob's sin which separated him, isolated him, and took him out from home. At the same time, everything which took place is embraced and provided for within the covenant purpose and the covenant love of God. God was to remove Jacob from a very dominating, domineering mother, the sort of mother who can ruin a promising son — and from a father who, though a believer, was gentle to the point of weakness and actually countered the revealed will of God. Isaac wrongly favoured, not Jacob, the son of promise about whom the Lord had said, 'The elder shall serve the younger', but Esau, the rough mountain man who, as the years went by, became a 'profane person'.

Jacob's lone experience has been our whole emphasis in this chapter so far. Now we move on to look at this incident in a slightly more expansive way. From the Setting of the Encounter, and the Solitude of the Encounter, we turn to:

THE STRIFE IN THE ENCOUNTER

Intervention by God

Jacob was alone, and yet he suddenly found that he was not alone. The truth which we have just been contemplating became vividly alive for him. He found himself alone with God. This is how it is put, 'And Jacob was left alone; and there wrestled a man with him until the breaking of the day' (v. 24). God has come into the picture now in a very definite way. He is here in the person of the Angel of the covenant as we have seen. This is a 'theophany', a pre-incarnation appearance of Christ in the form of a man.

The covenant God has once more broken into the personal experience of Jacob in a dramatic and sovereign way. Just as at Bethel twenty years before, it is God who has really taken the initiative. It is not said that 'Jacob was left alone and wrestled with a man'. It is put in such a way that there can be no doubt that this man came at him suddenly, and Jacob was surprised and arrested, engaged without warning in a struggle for his very life.

56

What we have seen already from the teaching of Hosea serves to remind us that prayer is at the very heart of it all. The terms used by Hosea to describe the prayer indicate a spiritual dimension to this physical struggle. Hosea writes of Jacob at this very point of his encounter with the Angel of the Lord that 'he wept, and made supplication unto him' (Hosea 12:4). At the heart of this titanic struggle is the reality of God's blessing this man. Jacob is so dealt with that he begins to hunger after what God has already determined to give him. Here lies the key to the entire encounter. It is the covenant God blessing his covenant child, fulfilling the very promise that Jacob had earlier pleaded before him, 'And thou saidst, I will surely do thee good' (v. 12).

Intimacy of the struggle

Although the physical aspect of the encounter is not its main importance, we must not eliminate the reality of the struggle as it is described for us in this telling little phrase, 'there wrestled a man with him'. This is not a 'vision of the night', nor is it a dream, such as the patriarch was given at Bethel. This is of a different order altogether. It is the drawing near of God, and Jacob is to have things unseen and eternal brought right into the immediacy of personal experience, the realm of the seen and the temporal.

As a matter of fact, the Hebrew wording probably has a nuance to it that the English translations do not, and cannot, convey. There is not only a sense of the tangible in this encounter, it is downright 'earthy'. There is no other word to describe what took place here. What that means is simply, that two strong men cannot lay hold of each other in wrestling and in combat and not be very deeply aware of themselves and of each other. Wrestling is, emphatically, a bodily, physical contest. The thought uppermost in the mind with the words 'there wrestled a man with him' must be how near God has come to this man — becoming like him, becoming one of bone and muscle and flesh, laying hold of him, exerting power upon him, using force against him. God is in the human realm here. That, of course, is a feature of redemption which was to be realized fully only in the incarnation of God's Son.

When we come to the Hebrew underlying the English word 'wrestling', we find something intriguing which points up this thought of earthiness. Many scholars trace the verb used in the Hebrew here back to the noun for 'dust', and so construe the verb as speaking, in a highly evocative way, of struggling and rolling in the dust of the encounter. Others prefer to link the word into a root which means to 'clasp', as wrestlers do. The source of the word does not really matter a great deal. Rather, what concerns us is the thought it conveys. Interestingly, it is used only in this story, and when spoken sounds very like the words 'Jabbok' and 'Jacob'. The necessary consideration for us is that there can be no doubt that it refers to a physical, hand to hand encounter that tested strength and sinew and muscle for Jacob.

Intentness of Jacob

'And Jacob was left alone; and there wrestled a man with him until the breaking of the day.' This solitary experience of Jacob's is suddenly invaded by the transforming presence and power of God. That is the theme of this verse, and indeed one of the main themes of the story. The Angel has come, and takes the lead in this incident in the night. He dominates the scene; he dictates the pace; he directs the encounter. Right through until 'the breaking of the day', Jacob is purely on the defensive. That is the sum of the story as it is introduced to us in its opening verse.

In the account there is a fascinating combination of Hebrew names which we have already indicated. At the outset we have the man, Jacob (*ya'aqob*); then, we have the name of the place, the ford Jabbok (*yabboq*); and then, finally, the ac-

58

tion of wrestling, or tripping a man by the heel (*ye'abeq*). Those names of similar sound attract the attention of the reader and, in themselves, begin to point up the lessons of the whole story. The Jabbok is on the border of the promised land. Before Jacob (a heel-catcher, a supplanter) may cross the Jabbok to a land of blessing, he must strive with God in order to enter in, and he must be blessed with the blessing of a new name (v. 28).

When we recall how Hosea speaks of Jacob's birth those linguistic links become highly significant. 'He took his brother by the heel in the womb, and by his strength he had power with God' (Hosea 12:3). When we lay that alongside the action and the words we have in our passage here, we begin to see that Jacob's wrestling is the culmination, the outcome, of the tendency displayed even before birth. The implication is that, because of the distinguishing grace of God, he was even then eager to grasp the blessings God was covenanted to bestow. Paul knew the same sort of compelling constraint: 'This one thing I do, forgetting those things which are behind, and reaching forth unto those things which are before, I press toward the mark for the prize of the high calling of God in Christ Jesus' (Philippians 3:13,14). Let us, in our day, seek God's blessing with the same urgency.

4

*'And when he saw that he prevailed not
against him, he touched the hollow of his thigh;
and the hollow of Jacob's thigh was out of
joint, as he wrestled with him'*
(Genesis 32:25).

This verse brings us to an intriguing and an important aspect of Jacob's encounter, that of his actual wrestling with God. It is this physical contest which lays the foundation for, and provides the pathway into, the second part of the experience, that of dialogue and verbal exchanges with God. So we focus now on the actual conflict into which Jacob was plunged when he found himself in the grasp of the Angel.

The text before us sets it all out very graphically. Its very words are expressive, 'prevailed . . . touched . . . out of joint . . . wrestled'. What strife, and energy, and strength, and endurance are all wrapped up in the picture they convey! God has laid hold of Jacob, and before the physical part of the encounter is over he is to be made very much aware that God has come and is dealing with him. To put it bluntly, it is the story of God crippling a man, the story of God assuming human form in order to lay his hand upon the man, and that in order to disable him.

Jacob had come on his outward journey with all the wonder of a new experience of God freshly stamped upon his soul. He had learned the nearness of heaven to earth, and the fact that God was with him. Now, those twenty years later, before he enters the land of covenant promise, God is going to give him other lessons, and teach him the danger of inward pride and the folly of going on in his own human strength. He is to learn that despite appearances, Esau is not his most formidable enemy. The Lord has a work to do in him that will turn his own strength into weakness, and make him learn from personal experience that when he is weak then he is strong (2 Corinthians 12:10). Wrestling involves contest, conflict, struggle.

John Calvin puts his finger on one of the central lessons of this experience when he says that it is a great 'specimen of the temptations' of the people of God in every age. All the servants of God are wrestlers in this world and will meet various kinds of conflict, and so whenever God brings our faith under test, he says, 'our business is truly with him, not only because we fight under his auspices, but because he, as an antagonist, descends into the arena to try our strength' (*Genesis*, p.195). Just as all our spiritual prosperity flows from God, so do our spiritual trials and difficulties.

Already we have looked at the Setting of the Encounter, the Solitude of the Encounter and the Strife in the Encounter. Now we proceed to gather up the suggestions of this verse by looking first of all at what it shows us of:

THE TOTALITY OF COMMITMENT

Probably very few readers of this book will have been in a wrestling contest but we have all seen wrestlers, perhaps on television. We have seen people, up there in the ring, laying hold of each other in ferocious fashion and then exerting their strength and their skill — doing it all the more lustily and heartily, perhaps, just because they knew they were wrestling on television. Or it may be that we have seen those huge fellows wrestling on the field of athletics. There was a time when I did a little wrestling at our Highland Games in the north-west of Scotland. It did not take long to discover a very elementary fact about wrestling which helps interpret this story of Jacob wrestling the Angel of the covenant. It is simply this; you cannot wrestle with a man and stand six feet away from him. You have to get right in there and come to grips with your opponent, and the quicker you get in and do that, then the better it is for yourself and your chances of survival and of victory. Wrestling requires total commitment. So does a life of godliness.

Then I discovered this also: when you are wrestling with someone and he takes a hold of you and he is seventeen or eighteen stone, you soon know that you are in the grasp of a mighty man! You know you are in for a struggle, and the only way to survive is to throw your whole heart into the contest and aim for nothing less than outright victory. A half-hearted approach will not do. It will endanger your very life and even the life and well-being of your opponent. What do you require in order to be a good wrestler? You need courage, and you need concentration, and you need strength, but above all you need enthusiasm and energy. You have to get in there and get on the attack with all your heart and soul. Let me illustrate what I mean.

The energetic attack

I remember a moment when I saw one of the basic principles of good wrestling given vivid illustration. An incident took place which drove home to me the importance of what the old wrestlers called 'energetic attack'. There, being watched by a vast crowd, on a lovely, sunny, July day on one of our West Coast islands, were two strong, fit chaps, wrestling on a sports field. One of them attacked so energetically that the other was able to concentrate only on defending his position. The attacker grappled his man, gave a mighty twist, and threw him to the ground. However, the other had been so intent on defensive action that he fell awkwardly, and the man who was throwing him actually fell on top of him. In fact, both took a heavy fall, and in the fall one of them was hurt badly. His leg was broken in that awkward fall, and you could, quite literally, hear the bone snap thirty yards away. He knew he was wrestling! He would tell you that he had been caught off balance, and that this was the result of concentrating on defence rather than attack.

The moral is plain. These lessons can be applied to the spiritual life, and they are relevant to much of our Christian experience. To be a Christian is to be caught up in a life of conflict and it is a life that makes great demands upon us as God drills us in lessons of humility, obedience, and trust. That being so, there are situations where we are much safer if we go into the attack rather than remain solely on the defensive.

Wrestling is a very good analogy of the spiritual life. Paul says to the Christians at Ephesus, 'We wrestle not against flesh and blood . . .' (Ephesians 6:12). The idea conveyed is one of conflict and testing, picturing a life which requires effort and discipline, and demanding that we 'work out' our salvation with much spiritual energy (Philippians 2:12). You cannot wrestle and remain 'uninvolved'. In the same way, you cannot come to grips with God and let God come to grips with you and not know about it.

The enthusiastic approach

To be a good wrestler a man needs to be very fit. That requires effort, regular training, and strict self-discipline. The athletes I knew when I was young spent hours running, working with weights, building up strength, improving muscle tone, sharpening physical speed and mental alertness. A wrestler needs to be very quick and very strong. His mind needs to be ahead of every single physical action. You might think when you watch the really big fellows on television that they are just all fat and muscle and very stupid. They are not. They have very quick minds and they are probably highly intelligent men. To be a good wrestler a man's mind must have the speed of lightning, his hands and feet must move very quickly, he must bend all his energies into the effort he is

63

making, straining every sinew and muscle and nerve, and he must concentrate fiercely all the time. Moments of defeat almost always coincide with moments when concentration is lost, even for a split second.

Danger always concentrates the mind. There can be crowds round about you but if you are trying to keep seventeen or eighteen stone from falling on top of you and breaking your leg, you forget everything — your circumstances, your surroundings, your ambitions — and you concentrate every thought, every muscle, every nerve just on what you are doing. There is only one other being in the world for you, and that is your opponent. It is the same with the soul who truly comes to grips with God. The immensity and the reality of God come in on him and that is one of the factors that transform the hearts of all who are confronted by God. They can never be the same again. The Lord Jesus becomes the all-important person, and living in obedience to him the all-important objective.

The earnest attitude

Although there are other matters involved in Jacob's experience, there is no doubt at all that this whole incident relates very closely to prayer. Because that is so there is one question that offers itself readily. It is very personal and hallowed, and belongs to that secret place of life, the relationship between your soul and God. It is simply this. Do you know, in your Christian experience, what it is to wrestle with God in prayer? Do you know what it is to go aside and be alone with God in prayer? Our forefathers did: they did it in Scotland and they did it in Wales, and they pulled the power of heaven down among men. They did! Our forefathers talked about prayer as 'wrestling with God', and they knew it as an experience of their Christian life.

We come now to a very important part of Jacob's encounter with God. In the text which heads this chapter we read that Jacob gave a very good account of himself against the Angel. When the Angel saw that Jacob was totally absorbed, and flinging all his energy and power into the conflict, and that against every tug and thrust he received, he still wrestled on, the Angel did something extraordinary and extremely significant. This is how it is put. 'He touched the hollow of his thigh; and the hollow of Jacob's thigh was out of joint, as he wrestled with him.' The Angel crippled Jacob, and he did it with only a touch.

THE TENACITY OF PURPOSE

One of the things we notice in this story is that the Angel, at the outset, refuses to reveal himself. The entire conflict goes on in the darkness, and the choice of the word 'man' to describe the wrestler who has suddenly grappled with Jacob and forced him into the testing encounter has a powerful effect. The word chosen transports us, the readers, directly into Jacob's situation. Initially at least, Jacob knew only that a powerful male antagonist had closed with him. In the first verse which tells us this there is no hint of anything more than a man — it could have been Esau himself for all we know, or for all that Jacob knew at first. For him, that situation prevails through long hours of struggle in the darkness. It is only as the day begins to streak the eastern skies with the first rays of dawn, that we learn that the opponent is more than a man. In verse 25 we are just beginning to learn the truth, at about the same time as Jacob himself is to learn it.

We read that this mysterious opponent saw that his efforts were unavailing. What a wonderful thing a tenacious faith is; a faith that will wrestle on through the long moments and hours of darkness. The older one grows in following Jesus, the more one is conscious of the difficulties that attend a life of real prayer, or of true godliness. One of the greatest difficulties of the whole experience of a prayer life is having the faith to persevere when things are dark. It is easy when circumstances are bright and when your heart is warm and when you are enjoying what you think is the blessing of God. Here is one who fought on and on, exerting himself through the strenuous hours of the night; the Angel could not master him.

The fact that it is night-time wrestling which we have here has a double significance. On the one hand, darkness conceals the adversary's identity, and on the other hand the fact that he wished to be gone by daylight proves that it was he who had planned the night visit. The fact that the wrestling lasted till the breaking of day suggests a long, indecisive bout which eventually achieved its aims. The protagonists were evenly matched; that is, until the Angel resorted to unusual tactics in order to get the result he wanted.

The persistence of faith

The fact that stands out here is this: the persistence with which Jacob fought off God. He reckoned this man an antagonist, and this determined the fierce energy in which he wrestled with God. The thought may even have been in his mind through those long, dark hours that he must overcome this enemy in order to be alone with God. Not realizing whom he had, he wanted to get away and down to real business; to lay hold of God and seek his help. This physical encounter was a barrier which must be pushed aside so that he could come into the place of prayer and intercession. Initially, although the 'LORD is in this place', Jacob 'knew it not'. Bethel, in the opening hours of the Peniel experience, is being repeated.

The entire scene is so different from Bethel that we cannot blame Jacob. No dreams, no ladders, no vision here. This is a place of struggle, and sweat, and flesh, and bone, and dust. It is one of the hard places of life that need determination, and resolve, and persistence in order to escape from it as quickly as possible. That persistence is the persistence of faith; there is not much doubt about it. Jacob is concerned to enter the land that has been covenanted to him by a covenant-making and a covenant-keeping God. So he resists to the uttermost any attempt to detain him. He will not be diverted. He is determined to possess what God has promised. No matter who the adversary may be he is not going to stop Jacob getting on to 'home ground'. Jacob is strong in faith, and his faith keeps him battling on for victory over his enemy.

That promise of entering and possessing the land has another important blessing attached to it. We are not sure exactly how Jacob became aware that the wrestler he was grappling with was more than man. It may have been the unusual strength and perseverance of the man over hours of conflict that alerted him. Be that as it may, he certainly became convinced of it when the Angel 'touched' him with what was more than an ordinary touch. We shall look at this in a moment but, first, let us examine the faith which maintained Jacob through the dark hours of conflict.

That Jacob was a man of true faith we know from the earlier prayer in verse 9 — reminding God that he was the God of his father Abraham, the God of covenant promise, and the God who had dealt with him graciously at Bethel. That is why this ought not to be regarded as the conversion experience of Jacob. In prayer he had addressed God very specifically as 'the LORD which saidst unto me, Return unto thy country, and to thy kindred, and I will deal well with thee'. He was not merely the God of his fathers, but the God who had revealed himself personally and graciously as Jacob's own God also. There is a danger of misunderstanding the words of verse 11, and thinking that Jacob was praying only out of a natural fear. 'Deliver me, I pray thee, from the hand of my brother, from the hand of Esau: for I fear him, lest he will come and smite me, and the mother with the children.'

We must remember, of course, that Jacob had been driven away from home because of the hatred of Esau. That reminds us of the significance of verse 12 — 'And thou saidst, I will surely do thee good, and make thy seed as the sand of the sea, which cannot be numbered for multitude' — because that verse shows us that the faith of Jacob is concerned not only with himself or with his wives or children. He is concerned with the pledge that God will give him a numerous posterity. This embraces the messianic promise, and Jacob is anxious about his place and part in the fulfilling of that promise, and reminds the Lord of it.

Such language takes us back to Genesis 12 and Genesis 17, and the covenant promise to Abraham, for Jacob's faith is concerned about the covenant promise of God, not just about immediate disaster at the hand of Esau. So there is something to admire here in this determination. Does your faith reach out with pain and concern over the glory of God and the glory of his covenant when you see the masses despise him and when you wonder if the day will ever come when the promise will be realized that the whole earth shall be filled with his glory? Is there a pain in your soul, do you hold on to God in the dark for the coming of that day and the fulfilling of that promise? Jacob knew something of that pain.

The proving of faith

In the words, 'When he saw that he prevailed not against him', we see not only the tenacity of faith but the trying of it also. God is going to prove his servant and teach him some important lessons about the life of faith through this night of strain and testing. Although he was already a man of God, the fact is that Jacob was all too prone (as we all are) to rely on the 'arm of flesh', on his own abilities. Therefore he had to learn (as we all must) that natural ability will not win spiritual battles. Paul put it like this: 'The weapons of our warfare are not carnal (not of this world), but mighty through God to the pulling down of strong holds' (2 Corinthians 10:4).

Once more, think of wrestling. Wrestling is the clashing of

physical power, the coming to grips with each other of two men. Behind the physical is something else. It is not merely the clash of bone and muscle — it is the meeting of two wills, and it is the attempt of one will to bend another will to its purpose. That happens in every wrestling contest, but the only way that the unseen thought is unveiled to the onlooker is in the ebb and flow of the physical progress of the conflict. On the surface of things, that physical confrontation seems all there is to it, but the deeper conflict is that of the mind and the will. This is involved here with Jacob and the Angel. It is a real, physical encounter. But it is more. This conflict touches the deep, hidden, basic realities of the spiritual life. It has to do with will and emotion and heart; with motive and purpose and prayer; with seeking the will of God; with knowing the will of God; with doing the will of God.

There is always the danger that in prayer we agonize in order to impose our will upon the sovereign will of God. Ask yourself a question. What do you think prayer is? Is prayer the attempt of the believer to bend God to do his will? To listen to many people praying that is what you would think prayer was, and to listen to some men preach about prayer you would think that was what prayer was. But prayer is in fact the very opposite. It involves putting oneself into the hands of God until one is brought to the place the Saviour himself once occupied: 'Father, if thou be willing, remove this cup from me: nevertheless not my will, but thine, be done' (Luke 22:42). It is when God has handled you until you say, 'Yes, Father, it is good' even when there is pain in it, that prayer has had its perfect work in you.

It is on the basis of that principle that we can see, at the deep level of prayer and the spiritual realities underlying the physical and the tangible, how God laid hold of Jacob in order to wrestle him into a place of light and of spiritual illumination. The place where God's light breaks into the soul of man is dangerous. The flesh does not like it; thoughts are revealed; the motives of the will, the plans of the heart are laid bare. The activities of the life are exposed, and one of the last things we wish, even as Christians, is that God should bring us into the place where his light shines in that fashion. That is especially true when we know that there is sin being harboured and indulged in our hearts and lives.

Jacob opposes all that the Angel does. Every turn is met; every twist withstood; every grip countered. Jacob was terrific at resisting. He had been well schooled in the theology that would further faith in the ways of the flesh. He had learned from his mother, and his mother had acted in the very way that Jacob was acting now. She had acted in the power of carnal wisdom in order to fulfil the covenant promise of God.

THE TOUCH OF THE ANGEL

There is one remarkable moment in the whole incident. It is the turning point in the wrestling contest, the moment when the entire conflict takes on a new aspect not just for the reader of the story but for the man who is the subject of the story, Jacob himself. It is the point at which we see God in the actual process of enlightening Jacob, and unveiling himself to him as the Lord. We read this: 'He touched the hollow of his thigh; and the hollow of Jacob's thigh was out of joint, as he wrestled with him' (v.25). He 'touched' him. It would require a very severe blow, or twist, to dislocate the thigh joint of a fit man; it would be highly unlikely to happen in an ordinary wrestling match, such is the violence required. However, the Hebrew text employs a mild term for this touch which, when compared with Isaiah 6:7, where the coal touched Isaiah's lips, indicates that it was probably just a touch of the finger rather than a fist. The word used, in this particular context, suggests that the ensuing result — the serious, crippling injury suffered by Jacob — had been brought about, in a supernatural way.

What a shock this must have been to Jacob. The incredible

had happened, and the one with whom he had been so strenuously contending was the very one he required to bless him and help him. All his struggling had only antagonized the Lord and now, here he was, wounded and helpless. This touch must have been the thing which first made him realize that his wrestling opponent was no ordinary man. It constituted a moment of revelation, confirming suspicions which had been crowding in on him and growing stronger as the hours went by. Until that moment they had been only suspicions. He was certain now; he knew he was in the hands of God. It was useless to contend further.

A gentle touch

This is highly instructive. It demonstrates the sheer grace of God in his dealings with us. God did not crush Jacob. He did not have him down in the dust and say to him, 'Jacob, feel my power, know the damage I can inflict, see how easily I can smash you.' He touched him very gently, and his power was more vividly demonstrated in that gentleness than it would have been in the greatest violence Jacob might have been fit to withstand. This is the wonder of saving grace. When God comes to deal with us in our darkness he comes so gently and tenderly. Touched — but why in the hollow of his thigh?

You will have noticed something very simple but interesting about wrestling. Even a little knowledge about it tells us that a wrestler depends of all things upon his thigh. Every single throw that a wrestler uses is a throw that centres around one pivot — the pivot of his thigh. If you want to destroy the power of a wrestler you injure his thigh, and he is finished. God just touched Jacob in the place of a wrestler's strength and Jacob was as helpless as a baby in the hands of God. Jacob, be still. Jacob, stop resisting. Jacob, be submissive and yield to the hand, yield to the touch. If I do this with one little touch, what will I do if I exert my strength against you? The most awe-inspiring thing for any wrestler to experience, and especially one tired and worn, is that he is in the hands of such strength that he might be a child!

A humbling touch

At that point, something died in Jacob — the pride of self. His self-confidence and self-reliance took a bad tumble. He was humbled. A wrestler has pride in his ability and when he is beaten he is humbled. Do you know what it is to be humbled by the finger of God? We hear much now about coming to Jesus and deciding for him and being happy and all our problems being over. There is little said about repentance, the need for God to work in us those graces which please him: 'The sacrifices of God are a broken spirit: a broken and a contrite heart, O God, thou wilt not despise' (Psalm 51:17). We need to go back to the doctrine and the teaching of our godly fathers. God is great and only God is great. Man is dust, and but for grace man would be destroyed. Our place before God is always a place of humility and penitence.

What happened at Peniel can be illustrated in this way. Jacob was broken in the place of his strength. What does a wrestler do if he gets a sudden injury to his hip? There is really only one thing he can do. He wraps his arms around his opponent and holds on as hard as he can. This is what was designed by the Lord. In one moment, Jacob was hurt and weakened, and made to cling to God as he had never done before. On the other hand, what does a wrestler do if the other man clings to him in this way? The only thing he can do, again, is brace himself, tighten his own grip, and bear all the weight of his opponent. The moment that happens, his thighs and legs become the pivotal centre of the conflict. So here, as Jacob is hurt and clings, the Angel's arms are wrapped around him, draw him close, support him, and the entire scene has changed yet again. All of a sudden, it is the pillars of God's strength that are upholding Jacob and sustaining the whole conflict.

A gracious touch

This is the very same lesson the apostle Paul was taught. Listen to him speak of the experience. 'There was given to me a thorn in the flesh . . . For this thing I besought the Lord thrice, that it might depart from me' (2 Corinthians 12:7,8). In fact it did not depart from him. He was to be left with his weakness and disability, and that weakness and disability would make him cling to God all the more closely. Paul learned this valuable lesson: 'And he said unto me, My grace is sufficient for thee: for my strength is made perfect in weakness.' From it he formulated what is one of the basic principles of the Christian life: 'When I am weak, then am I strong' (vv. 9,10). Yes! When he is weak in himself he is strong with the strength of omnipotence. This is the lesson Jacob is being taught at Peniel. God's strength made perfect in our weakness; here is the power we should be seeking from the Holy Spirit, the power we see brought into the experience of Jacob at this point of his encounter with God at Peniel.

We have the same principle taught in one of the Psalms. The psalmist says, 'He weakened my strength in the way' (Psalm 102:23). God does that with every one of us because as we go on with the Lord from the place of conversion we begin to be strong in ourselves and we forget that we need God's grace fresh every morning. God has to show us that we really are as weak as we ever were, if we try and serve him in our own strength. We need him, and the continual upholding of his strong arms. 'Underneath are the everlasting arms' (Deuteronomy 33:27). This is what matters. Get the everlasting arms under you in all you seek to do for him. This includes your prayer life, because it is only by God's grace that you will pray aright. It is only grace that will enable you to overcome the difficulties; it is only grace and power and strength that will make you a wrestler with God. Jacob learned much in the moment that God 'touched him in the hollow of his thigh'.

Two truths were revealed to Jacob as they had never been revealed to him before. First of all he was given a revelation of God's power; and then he was taught that he did not need to give God a helping hand. He learned a lesson that Abraham his grandfather could have given him; he learned that if you rested on the promises of God by faith and through faith, these promises were fulfilled. Do you know what is said of Abraham? 'He staggered not at the promise of God through unbelief; but was strong in faith, giving glory to God' (Romans 4:20). There is one thing that will honour God and that is the full faith and confidence of our hearts. If there is one in all the universe who deserves our trust it is the God of all grace.

THE TOUGHNESS OF TRUTH

'The hollow of Jacob's thigh was out of joint, as he wrestled with him' (Genesis 32:25). This is not mere repetition. Rather, it reflects the way in which the encounter proceeded after Jacob had known the crippling touch of God. It speaks of the patriarch's weakness, and the changed attitude with which the contest was continued. The strong man had been made weak, and the Angel had been proved strong, so the contest proceeded on new terms from this point. It reflects also the awareness that Jacob now had of the opponent being more than man.

The dominant thought in his mind now must be the divine power of the grasp in which he found himself. He now knew he was facing a far more formidable opponent than Esau. Here is one who is righteous and who deals in that scarce commodity, truth that is true — and consequently, because of our sin, truth that can be hard to encounter. The knowledge did not stop him; it spurred him on; he would cling and be upheld and trust in the strength of his antagonist. That he had been touched and not smitten to the ground encouraged continuation. Only it was a different conflict, a new contest now.

To wrestle when crippled is not easy. Let us hold hard to what is said here: Jacob was severely handicapped — it must be all over with him now. Truth has caught up with him, and truth has smitten him and proved too hard for him. Yet the words do not stop there — they go straight on, 'as he wrestled with him'. Touched, injured, crippled, but wrestling on still.

Facing truth is always difficult. The Word of God shows us our true selves, and when it does it cripples us. We find it hard then to press on with seeking God, or God's blessing. Nevertheless we have to seek him as the God of truth, and as we do we learn that grace never comes at the expense of righteousness. This is part of the lesson that Jacob is being taught at Peniel. Here we touch the wonder and glory of the gospel. The essence of the gospel is the doctrine of justification by faith in Christ alone. It sets man and his doing aside, and lays all of salvation upon God and his grace.

This is the gospel that Martin Luther rediscovered, the gospel that Calvin found expressed so clearly and strongly in the writings of Augustine, the gospel that moved Switzerland and the Netherlands and France and Scotland, back to the cross and to God in the sixteenth century. Paul sums up the wonderful gospel of justification by faith. God 'justifieth the ungodly' (Romans 4:5). He is 'just, and the justifier of him which believeth in Jesus' (Romans 3:26). 'By grace are ye saved through faith' (Ephesians 2:8), and we have to learn this lesson as believers day after day after day. 'Not of works, lest any man should boast' (Ephesians 2:9). Jacob is learning here in the darkness of Peniel that no flesh will ever glory in God's presence (1 Corinthians 1:29). He learns that contact with God can continue at all only because he is being held by God. His confidence, his self-reliance, his pride — yes, now even his hope of the promised land — have all been put out of joint and he is closed in entirely to trust in the Angel in whose hands he finds himself helpless.

THE TENDERNESS OF GOD

It is marvellous that God saves his people. It is more marvellous that he does so in a way that glorifies truth. Because salvation rests on what Christ has done, it sheds glory not on us but on the God of all grace. It magnifies the name of Jesus and makes a countless throng sing through the running ages of eternity, 'Unto him that loved us, and washed us from our sins in his own blood . . . be glory and dominion for ever and ever' (Revelation 1:5,6). The Christian delights to be saved in a way that is consonant with righteousness, in a way that will let the nature and the holy name of God be unspotted and unblemished for eternity. He safeguarded his holiness with the blood of his Son and he will not save one sinner at the expense of his truth.

The toughness of truth is shot through with the tenderness of God. When I think of Jacob wrestling on in weakness and being dealt with on the basis of truth, my mind goes back to something I once read in one of the sermons of Martin Luther King. He said, 'God has a tough mind and a tender heart.' That is true. He has the tenderness of grace to touch us without destroying us, and the toughness of mind to banish evil from our hearts and the world he has made. He loves equity and righteousness and truth, and yet it is he who drew redemption's plan and gave his own Son to fulfil it for you and for me and for Jacob.

The tenderness of God does an astonishing thing at Peniel. That crafty element in Jacob, characterized by the name 'heel-catcher', or 'supplanter', God grasped and disjointed. Painful, and yet tender, the experience leads to better things. If God is going to bless us, and if God is going to use us in blessing, he will do the same with us. He will take our pride and put it out of joint. We could all give a hundred illustrations of how God has sometimes taken our plans and given them a twist until they were out of joint in a way we never expected. Jacob never anticipated twenty years with Laban. He planned only a brief stay; when he saw Rachel he was willing to wait for a few years, but eventually it was more than twenty. God upsets our plans and sometimes when we look back we have to say 'Thank the Lord' for the change, even when it was hard to bear.

There is pain when God puts things out of joint for us. This must have been a sore experience for Jacob. Let me make plain to all, but especially to young people — your pride, your pride in your youth, your pride in what God has done already for you if you are converted, your prejudices, your plans for your life, your reluctance about study, perhaps about serving the Lord; all these things God will have to take and give a twist to them and put them out of joint. It will be as you continue with him then, in love, in humility, in service, in obedience, and in prayer, that you will begin to understand this experience and the manner in which it makes one cling to the Lord Jesus — 'Jacob's thigh was out of joint, as he wrestled with him.'

5

'And he said, Let me go, for the day breaketh.
And he said, I will not let thee go, except thou
bless me. And he said unto him, What is thy
name? And he said, Jacob'
(Genesis 32:26,27).

From this Peniel encounter between Jacob and the Lord emerges the encouraging truth that when we meet with God we come into contact not merely with a power but with a person. It is a person who speaks, and reasons, and communicates thought and idea, who indicates approval or anger and deals with us in justice or in undeserved favour. Impersonal power can be a fearsome and destructive element in life, but the manifestation of personal power will depend upon the purpose and disposition of the intelligence behind it. This is the atmosphere we breathe as we view Jacob wrestling with God at Peniel.

THE SIGNIFICANCE OF THE ENCOUNTER

Personal revelation

New elements in the contest between the wrestlers begin to unfold in the verses before us. The Angel who is holding Jacob so closely, supporting his weight, ensuring his ability to continue in combat, begins to reveal himself at a new, higher level. He begins to ascend from the physical plane to the moral and spiritual. As he does so, the combat, in a very real sense, intensifies and becomes a most personal and searchingly intimate encounter. Not only Jacob's body, but his heart and soul are being grasped and handled by the Angel now. All the energy and testing of the conflict are being applied to the inward life of Jacob.

One significant and beautiful aspect of having God reveal himself in this intimate manner is that it brings the assurance of living, not in the clinical, soulless universe of the atheist but in a world created and ruled by the living, loving God. To come to know this God in Jesus Christ is to be aware that he has a magnificent purpose of redemption and deliverance for the world of which we are a part. Where there is personal being there is thought, and emotion, and purpose. Into this realm we pass with Jacob, as we read the simple, but strikingly personal action the Angel took when Jacob clung to him with the urgency of a wounded wrestler. The Angel of the Lord spoke to Jacob. As he does so, Jacob is made aware, and so are we, that the encounter begins to take on a new perspective.

Personal relationship

In the realm of salvation we cannot know the power of God without knowing God himself, any more than we can receive a blessing apart from receiving God himself. Yet, there is always the danger, one fears, that we want God's power and yet do not hunger after God himself; or that we wish for God's blessing and yet do not desire what always accompanies it — the presence of the God who is of purer eyes than to behold iniquity. The power of God never comes without God himself, therefore the power that transforms means personal contact. It is marvellous that, as persons, our salvation centres in relationship with a personal God. There is not merely contact; there is communication and communion, and so the personal qualities of our nature are given recognition and brought fully into the experience. Grace does not deal with men mechanistically, as if they were robots.

There is something else which emphasizes the truth that personal revelation of himself is a large part of God's purpose in laying hold of Jacob at this time, and in this way. In verse 24 we saw how Jacob came to grips with God, or rather, how God came to grips with him. Although Jacob sought solitude, in order to pray and seek God, he was suddenly confronted by the Angel of the Lord and he was immediately in the midst of an encounter he had not expected. We have seen that the choice of the spot and the time belonged to God, rather than to Jacob. That is an important factor for interpreting this event, and all the gracious dealings of God with men.

Wherever there is saving encounter with God that encounter is always on the initiative of God. God appeared there, at the time and in the spot where the man turned aside to be alone, and it was God who withstood him and initiated the physical contact and struggle. He came to grips with Jacob, and inevitably when God comes to grips with a soul, that soul must come to grips with God. Just as God dictated the time, place, and beginning of the wrestling he dictates the time when and manner in which it will end. By then his present purpose with Jacob will have been achieved. This is where we have arrived in the narrative. The encounter begins to enter a new and different phase. It moves from silent contact into verbal exchange: 'And he said, Let me go, for the day breaketh.'

THE SYMBOLISM OF THE ENCOUNTER

The fact that the Angel begins to talk of daybreak draws our attention to a significant feature of the entire contest. We have noted it already, but we must look at it more closely. It is simply the fact that this conflict began in the dark, at dead of night. God intercepted Jacob in the darkness. This is not merely good background to heighten the literary effect of the story. It is not the powerful imagination of the author exercising his creative genius. This is the inspired Word of God and it is the record of something which took place in the life of this great man of God. We are dealing with an accurate account of a true historical event. While we must be very chary of over-spiritualizing all the details, there is no doubt that we are to be aware of the fact that it was a night-time encounter by the design of God.

Why the night?

There are doubtless some very practical reasons why the encounter took place at night. There was the need for God to take Jacob aside from everything else. The night was a convenient time. Probably there was also the intention that darkness should conceal the identity of the Angel, helping the process of teaching and moulding Jacob by encouraging him to struggle on in his own strength until the moment was ripe for the Angel to reveal exactly who he was. Jacob was to be brought to the very end of his own resources. He was to be made to cling to the Angel, as we have already seen. We must also reckon with the simple, sound, biblical reasoning of Exodus 33:20, where God declares that man shall not 'see me, and live'.

The frailty of sinful man disqualifies him from seeing God in all his glory. While this is a pre-incarnation appearance of the Son, the one on whom men can look and be safe, still Jacob himself seems to have been aware of the danger of looking on the 'face' of God. The fact that he has glimpsed that face in the new light of dawn and lived fills his soul with awe as he leaves Peniel. That so much of the encounter went on in darkness and was over before sunrise indicates that Jacob's fears were being accommodated and his faith being tutored. He would never lose his awe of looking upon God, and yet he was taught that when God came as man, men could look upon him face to face and be spared. It is not for his own sake, but for Jacob's, that the Angel says, 'Let me go.' The darkness has had its usefulness in God's purpose. If Jacob had perceived at the outset whom he was opposing so lustily the conflict would never have got under way. He would have given up at the start and never dreamed of handling his 'enemy' with such robust and persistent obstinacy.

The dominion of darkness

While we recognize all such reasons for the night encounter, we do not violate Scripture if we also recognize the symbolical significance of the night and the darkness, and the spiritual lessons which can be drawn from the fact that the contest took place in such conditions. Ultimately, where God has his dwelling, there is 'no night there' (Revelation 21:25), and whenever Jesus comes to men he comes as the 'Light' (John 1:7). Such factors remind us, too, that this encounter is not merely a physical one. God has come to bless this man and to deal with the deep, inward, dark places of the soul. When Jacob was left alone he was, spiritually speaking, in terrible darkness, full of fear and doubt. His entire household, even his own life — all was under threat; he needed, and was in fact seeking, light on his whole situation. He had done all he could himself and yet he felt there was something more to do. That was why he sought solitude. There was a darkness inside him that troubled him in a way that the darkness around him did not.

How often the Bible speaks about darkness as the very symbol of evil. Remember the teaching of the Lord Jesus: 'Men', he said, 'loved darkness rather than light, because their deeds were evil' (John 3:19). They loved the darkness lest their evil deeds should be exposed. Is there darkness in your spiritual experience? Then you must ask God to lay hold of you and in your darkness you must lay hold of God. At Peniel the Angel of the covenant, our own Lord Jesus (though not yet revealed under that name), took hold of Jacob in the darkness, and as soon as he held him in the darkness of the Syrian night do you know what was true? The light was beginning to shine in the darkness that was filling the heart and soul of Jacob. It was the apostle John who said of Jesus, 'And the light is shining in the darkness, and the darkness cannot quench it' (John 1:5, author's translation).

Because the strong Angel of God was present, there was hope for Jacob even though he was in the dark, and the dark was in him. So, if you are a believer in Jesus, there is hope for you, even if you feel that you are, for one reason or another, presently walking in darkness. Even beyond that, if you are unconverted and unbelieving, if your soul is as dark as the pit of hell, look away to Christ — he gives light, and when light comes into darkness there is hope! He is the light shining in the darkness.

The deliverance from darkness

As light, Jesus is the perfect reflection of the Father. That thought conveys a very beautiful picture of what God is like, and that picture is perfectly true, perfectly biblical: 'God is light, and in him is no darkness at all' (1 John 1:5). At Peniel, on the deep level of spiritual reality, God who is light was bringing the soul of Jacob into light, wrestling him into the place and the light of a new understanding of grace and of covenant mercy. He is to be brought into an experience where every sinful thought and word and action will be set in the light of blazing holiness and be rebuked and reproved.

By this means Jacob would see himself in a new light; in the light of the God who was revealing himself to him in this strange, unusual wrestling of the night. The Lord was going to deal with Jacob, and shine into his heart until he had been brought to the place where his very thinking and speaking and doing would stand out clearly to his own mind and his own understanding. That is always what happens when God comes to the soul which is in darkness. When he comes he brings light because he is light. That takes place each time God visits men with his salvation.

This doctrine is beautifully presented by the apostle Paul: 'God', he says, 'hath shined'. Where? 'In our hearts' — notice that he says 'in', not 'into'. God is shining right in the very place of our personal darkness. This is in order 'to give the light of the knowledge of the glory of God in the face of Jesus Christ' (2 Corinthians 4:6). The night-wrestling of Jacob bears a strong and strange resemblance to this. We have seen that the central truth of the entire experience of this encounter is that Jacob is 'blessed' of God. God's blessing comes in light and ever brings light with it. The fact is that by the time the night is passed over into day, Jacob knows deliverance, not of a physical, but of a spiritual kind.

Paul, too, had an encounter with Christ on the Damascus road. This was surely what was on his mind when he said, 'God hath shined in our hearts.' Paul could have said with Jacob, 'I have seen God face to face.' So can any soul who, through faith in Christ, has been brought 'out of darkness into his marvellous light'. This is the experience which evokes thanks 'unto the Father, which hath made us meet to be partakers of the inheritance of the saints in light: who hath delivered us from the power of darkness, and hath translated us into the kingdom of his dear Son' (Colossians 1:12,13). This is what was beginning to happen in the experience of Jacob at this point, the very point when the Angel began to speak. His word brings light wherever it comes. Now Jacob is hearing it and now, too, Jacob, who has been 'touched' in such a miraculous way that he knows his opponent is the Lord, is being told, 'The day breaketh.'

THE SPLENDOUR OF THE ENCOUNTER

The darkness is about to be swallowed up in the light of a new day. Just as the rays of the rising sun are lightening the skies so the light of God is beginning to shine in the heart of Jacob. How does that light reveal itself? It does so in the way that the first renewing rays of gospel light always do show themselves in the soul of man — by seeking more light: 'I will not let thee go, except thou bless me.' When the soul of any man gets to this place we can be sure that God's light has begun to penetrate. 'For ye were sometimes darkness,' says the apostle Paul to the Ephesian believers, 'but now are ye light in the Lord: walk as children of light' (Ephesians 5:8). Light brings light and then obliges men to walk in light. In essence, Jacob is being taught that lesson more powerfully at this stage in his life than he had been taught it even at Bethel.

How wonderful! How majestic! How glorious when the God of all grace comes down and lays hold of one like Jacob, and turns his darkness into light! 'For thou wilt light my candle,' says David the psalmist: 'the LORD my God will enlighten my darkness' (Psalm 18:28). Let us bring this truth, and the great spiritual reality of which it speaks, close to ourselves, into our hearts. Is it not amazing that the Lord comes and takes hold of people like us to do such a wonderful work in us? He grasps us in the darkness and wrestles with us (sometimes painfully, but always powerfully), wrestles us into the light that shines in the face of Jesus. What happens at daybreak? The shadows flee, realities stand out sharply, clearly, freshly; perspectives are adjusted and we look around us and are glad.

The need of perspective

One of the things I used to have to do when I was shepherding was go out after foxes. We had many foxes living wild in our hills which used to destroy the lambs in our flocks, and in the springtime we had to go hunting their dens — the rocks and the holes where they reared their cubs. Time after time I would spend a whole night sitting outside a rocky den with a shot-gun across my knees waiting for a dog or a vixen to come in to feed the cubs, and in this way hoping to get rid of the slayer of lambs. Usually there was somebody with me because up in those hills it was very eerie and lonesome; but I can never forget the difference that the streaks of a coming dawn made to the perspective when you were sitting, waiting for those foxes to return.

On such occasions, events almost invariably followed a set pattern, and those events shed light on this vitally important matter of perspective. Let me explain what I mean. In the dark you begin to see things! There I would be staring into the night, watching what seemed to be an extra dark patch, or the thickness or movement of some living object. Of course, I knew it was a rock because it was a rock through the day, and therefore it was a rock at dusk when the light was just going. But why did it become alive at night? All of a sudden, in the dark it seemed to be moving, and I felt like lifting the gun and firing at it. 'Oh, it's a fox!' It was just the restraint of common sense that told me, 'Don't do it. Don't do it until it moves a lot closer anyway.' What was happening? The darkness was destroying my visual perspectives and there is only one thing that could readjust them and that is light. This is what takes place when God shines in our hearts: 'In thy light shall we see light' (Psalm 36:9).

The source of perspective

Saving encounter with God must involve such enlightenment. It must involve a revelation of who and what God is, and it is only in the light of the knowledge of who and what God is that a sinner comes to a realistic understanding of who and what he himself is. These verses tell us how Jacob was wrestled to the place where he was willing to look at himself in the light of the nature and the character of the God who was perfect in holiness and who says, 'Be ye therefore perfect', and 'Follow . . . holiness, without which no man shall see the Lord' (Matthew 5:48; Hebrews 12:14)

It takes the light of God's Word, and the illumination of the Holy Spirit with it, to adjust the perspectives of life and to set them within the true dimensions of eternity. When we come to know our sin and our unworthiness before God it takes something more to get the perspectives properly adjusted. Then, it takes the light of the glory of God in the face of Jesus Christ to tell us that although we are nothing — like Jacob, just dust of this earth — and although we have lifted the heel of rebellion against God, yet the God of all grace has loved us, and there is light and hope and peace and splendour and glory for us in the Lord Jesus Christ.

The result of perspective

A new day brings new light; it sets out new perspectives and it brings in new hopes. It may be you know nothing about what I have been saying; perhaps you have never been converted. Perhaps, also, you are no longer young, perhaps you are old and you have not yet been converted. Do not give up. Be like Jacob and cry to God and say, 'I will not let you go unless you bless me.' There was a time when I used to say to people who were growing old in their unbelief, 'Now your chances are getting very slim and if you are not converted before you are thirty-three (the age at which the Saviour died) then your outlook is very poor indeed, and getting worse all the time.'

However, I changed my mind entirely on this matter. I was preaching sometimes in that strain and saying that solemn thing in the first years of my ministry, in the city of Aberdeen. I had reached this conviction because, at the time, I was seeing numbers of young people being converted, and I was upset because so many of the older ones were remaining, as I thought, strangers to grace and to God. Then the Lord sent me to minister in another congregation, in the heart of the great city of Glasgow and taught me a valuable and new lesson. He taught me that people of eighty and eighty-five and eighty-nine can be born again by the Holy Spirit of God. So even if your day has been long and dark it can have the splendour of salvation at the end of it. 'All manner of sin and blasphemy shall be forgiven unto men' (Matthew 12:31), said the Lord Jesus. None perish who trust him and he casts none away who seek him, irrespective of age.

A new day brings new hope. If you are young you have the whole day of your life in front of you. What are you going to do with it? Hand it over to God. Let him shape and mould it and put purpose and perspective into it. Let him make it useful for himself and fruitful in his service. The older person, also, can know a new day and a fresh impetus in his service for the Lord Jesus Christ. That is the lesson before us now whether young or old. There is not just the hope of a new day for Jacob now, there is hope of a new man in a new day. That is still the principle along which encounter with God operates. 'If any man be in Christ, he is a new creature: old things are passed away; behold, all things are become new' (2 Corinthians 5:17).

THE SOLEMNITY OF THE ENCOUNTER

We must avoid thinking that at this stage the encounter was easy for Jacob. It was not. Instead, it was stern and sore and tremendously solemn. He knew now that he was in the grip of God. He had been crippled and he had been made to cling with all his strength. Spiritually and physically, Jacob was now very near the end of his own resources. For a man like Jacob, proud, self-reliant, clever, and quick in his mind, this was a dreadful state in which to find himself. Just at this juncture his faith comes under another severe testing. Let us look at this more closely.

A broken silence

It is precisely at the moment when Jacob is in pain and clinging to God, with everything having gone wrong and all his plans shattered, that God utters those words which turn the encounter into a new channel, 'Let me go, for the day breaketh' (v. 26). The change is signalled, not merely by the Angel speaking, but also by the command he gives. If this were only a wrestling match between two men, it would be the loser who cried out to be released. Jacob would be ready to concede that the other had won the victory and he could do nothing more in the way of struggle or self-help. What is happening, then, when God seeks to be loosed? One thing is that the silence has been broken, and broken by the Angel antagonist. Communication has begun. But there is more than that. God seems to be acknowledging the tenacity of Jacob's faith and the way in which he has persevered through the long hours of darkness. This thought is confirmed for us by the words in verse 28, which show us that Jacob has, in fact, 'prevailed' with God.

It is possible, also, to regard those words as being a sort of final testing of Jacob's faith. He has prevailed through the long, silent hours of struggle, but the night has taken its toll and so has his virtual defeat at the hands of the Angel. 'Jacob, you might as well give up; you're really no match for me; you can see that, if I wish, I can destroy you in a moment. Lay aside your desires and your seeking and let me go.' If such is indeed the case, then we see how the testing does demonstrate just how strong Jacob's faith still is. Nothing is going to stop him; the Angel is going to be given an assurance that faith wants its full measure — 'I will not let thee go, except thou bless me.' This is the sort of faith, of course, which is pleasing to the Lord: 'And ye shall seek me, and find me, when ye shall search for me with all your heart' (Jeremiah 29:13).

The following words, 'for the day breaketh', seem to indicate, also, 'Jacob, go and put into practice what you've learnt in this encounter with me.' This supports the thought that God is testing Jacob's faith by the demand to end the contest. This is always God's way. He always tests faith before he blesses, just as he will surely test faith after he blesses. He is saying, 'Jacob, the contest is over. It is daylight now. You have lost a physical contest but won a spiritual battle. Go and put its lessons and its victories into practice as you meet Esau, and for the rest of your life.'

A broken man

In his helplessness, his spiritual nakedness, his brokenness, with all thought of conditions or personal merit demolished, Jacob wants God and he wants God in blessing. He is insistent and persistent as he denies the Angel's request. We may sum it up like this: Jacob is now willing to be wrestled out into the light and to have his mind and his heart and his life laid bare. He will take blessing now, not on his own terms at all but on any terms the Lord wishes to impose — he will pay the price of the closest scrutiny, allowing what David called 'his inward parts' to be exposed. Exposed to the eye of God? Yes, but also to the eye of his own soul.

Show me myself, O holy Lord;
Help me to look within;
I will not turn me from the sight
Of all my sin.
(Thomas B. Pollock)

God already knew the sin of this man. Now he was going to bring it out to let Jacob see it in a new light, and that sight would make Jacob more conscious than ever before of his own darkness, because it is only when you are brought to light that you understand what darkness is. Furthermore, it is only a knowledge of darkness that makes you love the light. Jacob is being brought into the light more directly than ever before, and as never before in the past, he is to be made willing to 'walk in the light, as he (God) is in the light'. That is the important thing. 'If we walk in the light, as he is in the light, we have fellowship one with another, and the blood of Jesus Christ his Son cleanseth (keeps on cleansing) us from all sin'

(1 John 1:7). That reference is not only to fellowship among Christian believers; it is fellowship, according to the context, with God 'the Father, and with his Son Jesus Christ' (1 John 1:3).

We close this chapter with the cry of Jacob ringing in our ears, that wonderful, woeful, wounded cry that rises out of a yearning and a longing to know more of God. However, there remain some things to be done in Jacob before the cry is finally answered. As we pause, I urge you, whoever you are, or whatever your circumstances, to make this cry your own. I invite you to do this especially if you are unconverted and your life has been unblessed, old or young. For the sake of your soul, you say it. Look up to God, lay hold on him by faith, and say, 'I will not, I will not let thee go except thou bless me.' Are you willing to lay all this aside as of no great importance to you? Are you content to go on unblessed of God? If so, what a terrible, what a tragic thing sin has done in your heart and life! Only true, God-given repentance will remedy it.

6

*'And he said unto him, What is thy name? And he
said, Jacob. And he said, Thy name shall be called
no more Jacob, but Israel: for as a prince hast thou power
with God and with men, and hast prevailed'*
(Genesis 32:27,28).

The verse preceding the words before us expressed Jacob's
determination as he refused to release his hold upon the
Angel. He had been taken to the place where nothing, ab-
solutely nothing, would satisfy his heart but that God would
bless him. I hope that every reader of this book has, in the
mercy and grace of God, been brought to the same place.
There is nothing whatever in life as important as this: that we
should know the blessing of the God who alone can bless, and
know that blessing no matter what else comes into our experience of life. To know the blessing of God is to be made
rich for time and for eternity. To be devoid of the blessing of
God is to be left in a darkness that will never be lightened but
will become deeper and deeper until it becomes that awful, in-
explicable thing that Jesus meant when he spoke of those who
'shall be cast out into outer darkness' (Matthew 8:12).

The teaching of Jesus on men being lost is very solemn indeed. On the strength of what he has said, we can be sure of
this: there is encounter with God which is not saving encounter. There is encounter with God which involves the
final, inescapable, and eternal awareness of his majesty and
his wrath. 'If I make my bed in hell, behold, thou art there'
(Psalm 139:8).

What we are concerned with, of course, is the type of encounter which saves and transforms. This is what we are looking at in Jacob. We hear from his lips the notes of true saving grace, the cry of a needy heart in defiance of the Angel's petition to be released. Now we proceed to look at the further steps of the route along which God leads him to the moment of blessing. As we do so, we are again conscious that we are moving from the physical to the spiritual. Let us pursue that matter.

THE SPIRITUALITY OF THE ENCOUNTER

This cry marks a great change in Jacob's attitude. We have seen him live and act in a way very unfitting for a covenant child of God. We have seen how astute, self-confident, and manipulative he was in former years. At Peniel the Lord has brought Jacob into the place of physical defeat and spiritual weakness where he is at the very end of all his own resources.

It must be emphasized that this is not always the interpretation given to this moment and this cry of Jacob. Probably the most common view of it is that in the bleak hour of loneliness and fear Jacob gathered up all the forces of his strength and laid hold upon the strange and mystic visitor, and mastered him with great spiritual energy and triumph. The passage is frequently read even from pulpits in such a way that the very tone of the reader makes this emphasis, bringing out a note of triumphant victory. The accents of the reader reflect determination, and confidence, and the uncompromising demand of a victor; 'I will not let thee go, except thou bless me.'

Our interpretation of this story, and especially our observations on the light cast on it by Hosea, lead us to the inevitable conclusion that such a view is entirely mistaken. From the fact that Jacob had been 'touched', and broken in the place of a wrestler's strength, that he had been made to cling, and that hurt and wounded, with limbs made useless for the task, he had continued the conflict only because of the mighty upholding arms of the Angel — from all those factors we know that this cry is forced out of him because of his felt weakness; for Jacob that is a new experience.

The condition from which the cry comes

If we lay alongside of that vivid picture the exact manner in which Hosea speaks of Jacob's prayer — that is, of this very cry — we begin to see things differently, and to hear another sort of music in its tones. The words were uttered in a voice choked with emotion. This man who, one guesses, had not shed tears for many years past, who had never shown any sign of spiritual weakness or self-doubt, was bathed in his own tears, torn with his own cries; 'He wept, and made supplication' (Hosea 12:4). The determination flowed, not out of a sense of strength but out of a consciousness of absolute weakness; melted, beaten, baffled, and feeling his utter helplessness, he cried, 'I will not let you go until you bless me.'

This is the hour of Jacob's inward defeat. He has found himself at last, in the hour of darkness, in the grip of a power which he cannot manipulate. God has laid hold of him in such a way that he knows the person in whose presence he has ever been. This is the very one whose power he thought he had been using, to his own great advantage, down through the years with Laban. Now he was learning a new lesson about the power which belonged to the Lord; he was learning who was truly master. He knows he needs God's blessing as he has never known it before. At Bethel the blessing had come unsought, unasked. This time matters appear in a completely different light.

The principles along which God works

It is likely that all of us, in our own way and according to our own ideas, want God to meet with us and bless us. But do we fully realize what we are asking for when we ask God to bless us? Especially when we put it so strongly as Jacob here, we are asking perhaps for more than we bargain for — asking for what may well be a sore trial. The fact of the matter is that what we are seeing here, in the way the Lord is handling Jacob, is not just something which belongs only to an ancient story. Although it all may seem very alien to anything God's people are called on to experience nowadays, there are clearly drawn parallels. We must remember that Jacob stood right at the beginning of God's deepest revelation to men, and that he had only a brief, if vivid, spiritual and revelational tradition behind him. When we grasp this fact, we begin to understand that what we have to experience within us, had to be grounded in a more external, physical expression for Jacob.

However, irrespective of the differences there undoubtedly are, the Lord deals with us on the same principles which emerge in his treatment of Jacob. When God deals with Jacob in bringing him further along in his experience of grace, he works on the principles of grace — those basic principles according to which he deals with every single one of his people in every age.

We might think that when Jacob has been brought to the place where he cries to God out of an overwhelming sense of his need, he has arrived where the Angel had planned to take him from the very outset. Jacob sees that God wants to leave the scene. That urges him on to cry the harder. This is not strange if we pause to think about the condition in which he finds himself. 'I will not let you go, unless you bless me.' 'Lord, how can I afford to let you go? You have crippled me. You have left me useless in the face of my brother's advance; you have literally handed me over as a victim to his anger; you cannot desert me now — please!' Is the Lord really finished with Jacob at this stage?

The answer, of course, is No. We are aware that there are further steps to be taken before the blessing is actually granted, and Jacob's worst fears are laid to rest. Jacob has to be tested in other ways yet, and has to learn other lessons still.

THE SELF-RECOGNITION THROUGH
THE ENCOUNTER

It is at this stage that God does something entirely unexpected. He speaks and he asks, 'What is thy name?' Of course, we know that this question is not asked because God does not know whom he has in his grasp. Nor is it merely a rhetorical question. It has tremendous significance attached to it. It is not for the Angel's sake, but for Jacob's that the question is put. Neither is it merely a stratagem, such as we might use ourselves, to get another talking and into conversation with us. It is far more than this. When we ask, 'What is your name?' what we are asking for is a sort of personal disclosure from the individual, a self-exposure. That is precisely what God is doing here with Jacob. He is saying to Jacob, 'Who are you?' and the design of the question is to get Jacob to think, as well as to talk.

'What is thy name? And he said, Jacob.' That is a very significant answer. Already, just because we are so familiar with what the name Jacob means, we can see reasons why God puts this question. This would have been especially so in Jacob's own day, and indeed, all through the Old Testament era, when names were considered to be expressive of a person's character. They indicated not merely who a person was, but what the person was. Who are you? I am Jacob, the 'supplanter'; the 'heel-catcher'; the 'twister'; the 'wily one'. This was a confession of the kind of man Jacob was.

Jacob had felt reluctant to face Esau. In his unwillingness there is a hint that he had felt reluctant to face the past. This was what had been marching down upon him, with every appearance of threatening to destroy him. In turning to seek God in solitude and prayer, he was really attempting to evade the past and the drastic consequences it held for his present and his future. Now, just as he thought that in submission to God he had achieved that aim, the Angel was taking him out from the present moment and back into the past: it all focused very sharply in the utterance of that single word, 'Jacob'.

Isaac and the blessing

Even as he spoke his name and so confessed what he was, as he uttered the word 'supplanter', the echo of his previous word still rang in his own ears — 'except thou bless me'. His mind must have raced back into the past with the speed of an arrow. Where did it take him? Back to the old home in Beersheba, to the familiar scenes and the familiar faces, Isaac and Rebekah — and Esau! Relentlessly back to Esau and the guile with which he had bought the birthright and then, later, deprived him of the blessing.

As the question of the Angel hung in the air, Jacob remembered hearing it all before — in the very same words, more than twenty years previously. He had gone into a darkened chamber, where the aged Isaac was waiting expectantly for Esau and the marvellous meal at which Esau, with his culinary expertise, was so good. Fearing that death was not far off, and having at last come to a final decision, Isaac was all ready to pass on the blessing, not to Jacob the son of promise, but to his own favourite Esau.

That was the point at which Jacob had gone in to his father, after the most careful and deliberate preparations on his own part and that of his mother. He had gone in, and he had said, trying to disguise his voice as he spoke, 'My father' (Genesis 27:18). The old, blind man had turned, and with a puzzled frown had said, 'Who art thou, my son?' Jacob remembered now, also, the thing he had forgotten over the years. He remembered how he had said, 'I am Esau thy firstborn.' There had had to be another lie, as well; this time, one which had involved God. When his father had said, 'How

97

is it that thou hast found it so quickly, my son?' Jacob, in a moment of quick, smart thinking, had utilized the piety of Isaac's heart in the most blatant fashion to quieten his queries and allay his suspicions, 'Because the LORD thy God brought it to me' (v.20)

Then there had been that awful moment when, still puzzled almost to the point of disbelief, the old man had said to him, 'Come near, I pray thee, that I may feel thee, my son, whether thou be my very son Esau or not' (v.21). This was why his mother had dressed him in the rough, hairy goatskins — she had anticipated just this moment. When the old hands had held him tightly and moved over his shoulders and his neck and his arms, Isaac was deceived because those hands felt not the 'smooth' Jacob but, as he was persuaded, the rough Esau. Still there was the frown — 'The voice is Jacob's voice, but the hands are the hands of Esau' (v.22). Being persuaded, Isaac had blessed Jacob and then, Jacob remembered, the question had come once more, hesitant, fretful, undecided, 'Art thou my very son Esau?' Jacob had had to repeat the lie once more, the lie that had secured him the blessing: he had said, 'I am' (v.24).

Now he was being asked that question yet again — 'What is thy name?' and he knows that he cannot deceive those divine hands that hold him, nor look into those Angel eyes and tell the lie once more. 'What is thy name?' 'Who art thou, my son?' — and now, twenty years on he can no longer tell the lie; he cannot say, 'Esau', he can only weep out the single word, 'Jacob'. He can no longer seek a blessing on the basis of a lie. He wants the blessing, but he is willing to have it, now, on the basis of truth. That is the only way God does bless men, on the basis of truth. It is when we confess what we are — sinners, lost, needy, helpless — that God promises to bless us. Jacob now pleads no birthright privilege, true or false, to obtain God's blessing. He simply confesses what he is.

Esau and the blessing

The question must also have reminded Jacob very vividly of Esau. As he owned himself to be Jacob, he must have remembered his brother's bitter words over the accuracy with which he had been named at birth. Esau had uttered them when he discovered that Jacob had deceived Isaac into giving him the blessing. 'Is not he rightly named Jacob? for he hath supplanted me these two times: he took away my birthright; and, behold, now he hath taken away my blessing' (Genesis 27:36). For those men in their time, a person's name was indicative of character, and in every age character is important for men's relationship to God and to one another.

R.A. Finlayson, Professor of Systematic Theology at the Free Church College, Edinburgh, a masterly preacher and Bible teacher, used to say to us students, 'Gentlemen, the Bible teaches that, ultimately, character is destiny.' He then used to point out that one of the most important things that God's grace does is to change the character of those in whom it works. In this episode, Jacob is undergoing a character-moulding experience of God's saving power. He is made to look back, and the inherent sinfulness of his nature is brought home to him in an unforgettable way: 'I am Jacob — and I am well named. My life and my actions, as I look back, tell me that the only favour I can seek from God is unmerited; God must deal with me on the basis of his mercy. Because I am "Jacob", I am at his mercy'. That was true, literally as well as spiritually.

Jacob would recall not merely the way in which he had procured the blessing but the way in which he had obtained the birthright. To understand what was involved in that aspect of Jacob's past, the past with which God is now confronting him in no uncertain measure, it will help us to go back into the earlier history of Jacob and notice one or two things about the birthright and the blessing. For it is there that the beginnings of the conflict between the brothers lie, the conflict which is to be resolved only after this greater conflict with the Angel at Peniel. That reconciliation is recounted in Genesis 33:15-20.

Rebekah and the blessing

One of the important things to notice from the past is that Isaac loved Esau, and favoured him above Jacob. We are told, 'And Isaac loved Esau, because he did eat of his venison: but' — and this is an indication of how far back the conflict between the two boys goes — 'Rebekah loved Jacob' (Genesis 25:28). It would seem that their mother never forgot what the Lord had said to her when, conscious of some sort of conflict in her womb, she sought the Lord and was told, 'Two nations are in thy womb . . . and the elder shall serve the younger' (v.23, cf. Romans 9:12). This was why she loved Jacob. In other words, she believed what God had said, and acted on the belief that the birthright was covenanted not through Esau and to Esau, but through Jacob and to Jacob.

In the society and times in which Jacob lived the birthright was a very precious advantage. It carried the excellency of dignity and power with it; and it was especially precious in the family of Abraham because of the covenant promise of God. It brought a double portion with it in that family; it had spiritual power as well as temporal privilege. Spiritually it bestowed priestly rights within the family of Abraham and was the portion of the heir who would carry on the line of the promised seed — that abiding spiritual heritage, the line of which Christ would come.

Isaac knew of the promise, yet he loved Esau. Why? Isaac loved Esau because he ate Esau's venison! He is allowing earthly, material considerations to come between him and the bestowal of the blessing upon Jacob. Poor Rebekah has sometimes been treated harshly by preachers for her guile in acquiring Isaac's blessing for Jacob. No doubt she was blameworthy, but her actions flowed out of her faith and her longing to see God's promise fulfilled. The motive was good, even though the method was wrong. Isaac was much more to blame. He had allowed himself to become something of a hypochondriac, careful about going out, careful about eating — and he had fixed all his hopes on Esau.

The story of how Esau sold Jacob the right of the elder son in exchange for a meal is familiar to Bible readers. Neither Jacob nor Esau comes out of the transaction blameless (Genesis 25:29-34). Esau was ready to throw away the spiritual heritage for a good bowl of lentil soup. He placed little value on it. That is why, as we have seen, Scripture calls him a 'profane person' (Hebrews 12:16). He treated the promises and the privileges of God's grace disdainfully. He weighed them in the balances of this world where material advantages prevail and by its standard he found them wanting.

The shrewd Jacob is not without fault, either. Although he has a high regard for spiritual things, we find him offering here to buy something that God has promised in grace — without money or price! The birthright was covenanted even before his birth. This was something he needed no guile to win. That is important for us all. Just like Jacob, we too can be guilty of trying to buy blessings that God gives graciously and freely. That is true of every soul that seeks to be saved by works, and it is sometimes true of the way in which Christians seek God's blessing.

We do not read that Rebekah played any part in the birthright incident, but she certainly did in the case of the blessing. 'And Rebekah spake unto Jacob her son saying, Behold, I heard thy father speak unto Esau thy brother . . . Go now to the flock . . . and I will make . . . savoury meat . . . and thou shalt bring it to thy father' (Genesis 27:6-10). She put Jacob up to cheating his father and obtaining the blessing. As with the birthright, Jacob did not wait for God's time. He joined forces with his mother to manipulate matters, even though they were in the covenant promise of God. Although having the promise of God, mother and son together decided to help God along by carnal means, that is means suggested by their own wisdom and opportunism. With every one of us the danger to do that is always there. How often do we try to further the interests of faith with the weapons of the world?

No return

All this must have flashed through Jacob's mind as he told the Angel who, and what, he was. Perhaps for a moment there was hesitation. If there was it did not last long. He had been brought to the place where he knew that only trust in God could help him.

Behind this encounter, and the course it has followed thus far, is Jacob's self-confidence and his conviction that he will really be able to handle Esau. After all, Esau is not all that bright; Jacob has mastered him at every turn in the past. It is not just Esau, of course, it is those four hundred men he has with him. But, if the worst should come to the worst, Jacob still had one course of action open to him, he could take to his heels and get out of it all as fast as his legs would carry him. Now, however, even in the face of all his fears there was nothing left for him but dependence upon God — 'I will not let thee go, except thou bless me.'

We remember that Jacob was hurt; he was hurt in the place of a wrestler's strength. Now his pride, his plans, his prejudices, all were broken as they had never been broken before, and he came to what the old preachers used to speak of as 'the end of himself'. It was not just that he could no longer wrestle. He could no longer even run. He was to leave this place limping (v. 31), his legs no use now even as a means of rapid retreat. God had taken away every last vestige of hope in his own abilities that he might have felt. This is very humbling for Jacob. Indeed, it is very humbling for us all. We can only look at Jacob as he clings to the Angel of the covenant and say, 'How are the mighty fallen!' (2 Samuel 1:19).

Yet, what a place in which to be! What a position from which to hope! Closed out from every other prospect of help but that which comes through Jesus, the Saviour. He is at the end of himself. But when he is there, he has found the only place of peace that a sinner can know in this world.

THE SERENITY ATTAINED IN THE ENCOUNTER

Conviction of sin — the beginning of the end

This is a great and encouraging truth. When God brings us in our longing and desire for blessing to the end of ourselves, we are at the beginning of God. This is where Jacob is now. We find his situation reflected in the lives of many of the saints in the Bible.

For example, in one of his great psalms we see David looking up to God out of a similar helplessness — and out of a great sense of personal need. David has been a man of God for many years, but even so has fallen into the sins of adultery and murder, and in Psalm 51 we find him looking up to God, terribly convicted of his fault and its evil. He prays, and in essence he is praying the same prayer as Jacob prays when he pleads for the Angel's blessing. Out of the anguish of his failure, David calls directly from the inner depths of his soul, 'Create in me a clean heart, O God; and renew a right spirit within me . . . Restore unto me the joy of thy salvation' (Psalm 51:10,12).

Confession of sin — the basis of blessing

We know from the New Testament how important it is to confess our sins to the Lord: 'If we say that we have no sin, we deceive ourselves . . . If we confess our sins, he is faithful and just to forgive us our sins, and to cleanse us from all unrighteousness' (1 John 1:8,9). This is the point to which grace will inevitably bring the erring believer. Although not a

103

pleasant place to be it is the one place where restoration into peace will begin.

One of the great paradoxes of the Christian life is the fact that when we despair of finding peace from any resources within ourselves, we look out to Christ and his finished work and there we find a pardoning God. It is then, and only then, that peace begins to come back into our hearts. It comes from the God who has made peace through the blood of Christ (Colossians 1:20). This is the only way for us to regain peace if, by our own foolishness and sin, we have forfeited it. Have you lost the joy that once you knew? Has some sin, perhaps that of sharp practice as with Jacob, or of immorality or adultery as in the case of David, robbed you of your peace and blessing, so that for long you have been walking on in your own resources? Do you feel as William Cowper did:

> *Where is the blessedness I knew*
> *When first I saw the Lord?*
> *Where is the soul-refreshing view*
> *Of Jesus and His Word?*

If this is the case with you, what should you do? You should do what Jacob and David, and many another sinning, backsliding Christian have had to do. You should seek the Lord with all your heart and implore him to restore you.

God is bringing Jacob out into the light and Jacob is being made to face himself. Even after years of Christian experience God does that with us again and again. Such sin is sin against light, and it is always a terrible thing to see oneself in the light of God's holiness. Yet it is the only pathway back to restoration and to serenity in our walk with God. This is part of what the Lord is doing with Jacob at Peniel. The 'heel-catcher' is crippled and is required to confess his true nature before he can be blessed. He will be blessed, not on his own terms, but on those laid down by a righteous and holy God. The question 'What is thy name?' had taken Jacob back over

104

the way he had come in his life's pilgrimage. It also prepared him for what was yet to come, for the blessing the Angel of the Lord was going to give him.

THE SEAL GIVEN IN THE ENCOUNTER

When Jacob confesses his name, the response of the Angel is immediate and authoritative. All the indications are that, spiritually, the conditions are now fulfilled on which God's blessing is to be imparted. As a proof of this, and for his encouragement, the Angel now says, 'Not Jacob shall your name be called from now but Israel, for you have fought with God and man and have prevailed.' Jacob is being taught that his real character is not the one that the events of unregenerate days suggest but the one that the contest and contendings of this momentous night indicate. Those events, and the renewed nature they authenticate are to be enshrined for evermore in this new name 'Israel'.

Israel — derivation of the name

Israel is a very interesting name and its precise meaning has caused, and still causes, a good deal of disagreement amongst biblical scholars. For long, it was thought to centre in a word the root of which suggested the meaning to 'rule' or 'judge' or 'be lord over', and so we had the translation 'prince of God'. However, when the name is analysed in terms of the strict meaning of its parts, and the interpretation given by the Angel to Jacob is added, some very interesting and suggestive ideas emerge. It is hardly possible to be certain about these but let us look at some of them, considering first of all the actual name as the Angel pronounces it to the broken, clinging Jacob.

A simple analysis of this is straightforward. The first letter in the name 'Israel' denotes the third person singular, 'he'; the middle syllable comes from a word which means to 'fight' or to 'contend' or even, to 'wage war'; and the last syllable is *El* the Hebrew name for God. So, combining the significance of its constituent parts, we see that 'Israel' means, literally, 'God contends', or 'God fights', or 'God wages war', or 'God struggles with'. This fits in well with all that has taken place at Peniel. God has come in human form and he has come as 'a man of war' (cf. Exodus 15:3). He has laid hold of Jacob, and although he has tempered his power to suit Jacob's strength he has, after hours of struggle, made his power evident in a touch. The difficulty commentators feel here is simply, how can this name be applied to Jacob? Many feel that it is best to take the inferential meaning, and read the name as 'He contended with God', even though there is no actual word for 'with' in the name.

Support for this way of reading the name is sought in the explanation which the Angel gave in his additional remark to Jacob — a remark regarded as expository of the name — 'Thy name shall be called no more Jacob, but Israel: for as a prince hast thou power with God and with men, and hast prevailed.' But the problem is not wholly solved, for this explanation also has difficulties, not least of which is the fact that, if the name means 'God fights', then its meaning has to be reversed in order to make it say that Jacob fights with God.

However, a common feature of Genesis is the way in which the narrative frequently makes use of a loose play on the sound or meaning of words and names in order to express their significance. We have seen this even in the name 'Jacob' and the similar words which are used right through the passage. Where his name formerly emphasized his character as 'deceiver', or 'supplanter', his new name is to emphasize the persistence which grace has imparted to him all along, but which it has now brought into the forefront of his life through this very encounter. Hosea's use of the incident seems to confirm this for us — 'Yea, he had power over the angel, and prevailed' (Hosea 12:4). The interpretation of the Angel confirms that, as Jacob was the object of God's 'wrestling' and 'contending' through the contest which is just ending, so God had been the object of Jacob's own struggles and contendings. The name Israel would always recall the event in which Jacob wrestled with God and prevailed. It was to be the lasting seal of this great experience for Jacob's own heart and for the generations that would follow in the covenant line.

Israel - connotation of the name

There can be little doubt that the primary element in this new name, and in Jacob's becoming Israel, is the purification of character. It has to do with sanctification, with consecration, with godliness of life. Peniel marks the triumph of God's grace over the self-reliance and pride of Jacob. In a very real sense the outcome of the match is a paradox. The man who is broken and has to plead for a blessing in defeat is Jacob, and victory belongs to the Angel. Yet, out of the ashes of defeat comes Israel, a man who has been made strong in grace and power with God.

Nevertheless, we must take account of the fact that the victory of this night is not complete, or static. Reflecting the experience of God's people in every age, there are times still when the old Jacob is to predominate over the new Israel. It is noticeable that through the remainder of Genesis the name Israel does not completely displace the name Jacob. Representing a personal achievement, and a spiritual disposition, it is used interchangeably with Jacob according as the newer or the older aspect of the man is in the ascendant.

Let us observe one more feature about the phrase 'hast thou power . . . with men, and hast prevailed' (v. 28). Hebrew has a strange idiom here, which makes the second verb future. God is saying, 'Jacob, you have shown that you can contend with God. How much more will you in future contend with men!' This suggests that the name 'Israel' is not exclusively tied to the man but also anticipates the time when the nation would be called by that name, and that God is speaking of the victories which the nation, and even 'the Israel of God' (Galatians 6:16), shall win. The church of God needs power. As witnesses of the gospel we need power with men. We want to be able to influence men for God. All preachers want power with men for God. Notice the way it is put here: 'hast thou power with God and with men'; and there is the divine order. Preachers will have power in the hearts of men when they have power in the presence of God.

THE SOUL MATURED THROUGH THE ENCOUNTER

Another arresting paradox of this passage is that the victorious Israel who comes away from Peniel comes limping out of it on a dislocated hip. We shall look at this more closely later, but there is no doubt that this is one of the principles of the work of sanctification. It weakens dependence on nature, and casts the soul over on to dependence on God. When the touch of God shrivelled the strongest sinew of Jacob the wrestler, it did exactly the same thing to his persistent self-confidence. His carnal weapons of warfare were left lamed and useless; they proved totally inadequate for his struggle with God. The belief which had been growing in him ever since Bethel dawned in his soul now with a new clarity: he was in the hands of a God against whom it was useless to struggle. Crippled in his natural strength, he had been made bold in faith; changed from a 'Jacob' into an 'Israel'. At Peniel Jacob experienced what Jesus had in view when he said, 'Whosoever shall lose his life shall preserve it' (Luke 17:33).

'Character is destiny.' Here at Peniel God is doing something new in the character of Jacob. It is not regeneration which is involved, but a step forward in sanctification. Some have preached that this was the conversion of Jacob. However, the prayer of verses 9-12 in this chapter, and other

108

features of his story in Laban's land, indicate rather that not Peniel but Bethel was the real regeneration or conversion experience. Spiritually, Peniel marks an advance on Bethel. 'Thy name shall be called no more Jacob, but Israel' — 'Now your character will conform to your status. You will be truly a new man.'

The Angel was reminding Jacob of what regeneration really is and what it involves. We go back to our overall theme, that of saving encounter with God. What does it do? It makes new creatures in Christ Jesus. When we are new creatures in Christ Jesus 'old things are passed away' and 'all things are become new' (2 Corinthians 5:17). Then, through the process of sanctification we are brought into conformity to Christ. It was Paul who spoke of the new creation. It was also Paul, himself a new man, who said this: 'Not as though I had already attained, either were already perfect . . . but this one thing I do, forgetting those things which are behind, and reaching forth unto those things which are before, I press toward the mark for the prize of the high calling of God in Christ Jesus' (Philippians 3:12-14).

7

'And Jacob asked him, and said, Tell me, I pray thee, thy name. And he said, Wherefore is it that thou dost ask after my name? And he blessed him there. And Jacob called the name of the place Peniel: for I have seen God face to face, and my life is preserved'
(Genesis 32:29,30).

We have come to where the encounter reaches its high point and Jacob, being blessed, goes out from a place which he will never forget. The situation prevailing at the beginning of the contest has been completely reversed. The self-confident child of covenant grace has been subdued by his covenant God. He had been so handled that he had been made to look into his heart with searching and humbling self-scrutiny. Jacob had contended, and his contending had been consummated in total submission. This is reflected in the question he asks, and he asks it, perhaps, a little anxiously, 'Tell me, I pray thee, thy name.' He is acknowledging the other's mastery over him. Submission of this kind involves rule, and duty, and obedience. Already, as he asks the question Jacob knows in whose hands he is. It is the God of Bethel and he is ready to submit to God. Here is one of the key themes in this story, and in the life of godly obedience.

THE SUBMISSION IN THE ENCOUNTER

There are five possible conclusions to any wrestling bout. The first is the best of three falls. Here, the wrestler who holds his opponent down for a certain length of time on two occasions wins the bout. The second possible verdict is a knock-out. It does not often happen but when it does, the loser is usually unconscious or badly hurt. The third is a draw, when the strength and skill of the wrestlers are so equally matched that neither one can gain the upper hand. The fourth is the verdict of submission, and the fifth is disqualification, when one of the contestants is guilty of unfair conduct. As Jacob asks for the Angel's blessing, he does so in a spirit of submission. In wrestling, a submission always comes because the one who submits is no longer able to strive; he has been rendered helpless. The rendering helpless of a wrestler who submits is usually very painful, and Jacob had a painful experience. We have seen something of that. He was wounded and hurt in the place of a wrestler's strength, and he had to cling.

One thing which perhaps escapes the onlooker, but was certainly true of the wrestling at our Highland Games, was this. When one man submitted because of injury or because of a hold which was going to lead to injury, the opponent was always very gracious. In the incident related earlier the one who had broken his opponent's leg was far more anxious and concerned than the one who was hurt. This may not always be true among men, of course, but it is certainly true of God. We see it here. We can see, in the tenderness of the grace of God with Jacob, that he wounds only to bring into complete submission. It is the submission of trust; and it is that trust which God is pleased to bless. Jacob has been learning an awesome lesson, that he must trust this adversary who has mastered him completely and utterly. It is in the light of this that he says, 'Tell me . . . thy name.'

Why did he ask God his name? The fact that he had just been made to confess his own name was still fresh in his mind, and the power of suggestion arising from that must have been strong. This is especially so when we recall what has already been mentioned, how in the Hebrew idiom the name is the index of character and personality. We have seen that names in Scripture have great significance — a person's name stands for his character. Jacob is seeking to know more of this divine person who, in such a short time, has wrought such overwhelming changes in his thought and in his heart. John Calvin says on this. 'It is not to be wondered at, that the holy man, to whom God had manifested himself under so many veils and coverings, that he had not yet obtained any clear knowledge of him, should break forth in this wish: nay, it is certain that all the saints, under the law, were inflamed with this desire' (*Genesis*, pp.200-1).

Progressive revelation

It is Calvin, too, who draws attention to the same question on the lips of another Old Testament saint, Manoah. In the Book of Judges we read of a similar appearance of the divine person who wrestled with Jacob, the Angel of the Lord. Unaware of the identity of this person, Manoah asked the same question as Jacob: 'What is thy name, that when thy sayings come to pass we may do thee honour?' (Judges 13:17). To this query he received the same answer as Jacob, 'Why askest thou thus after my name,' with this additional comment, 'seeing it is secret?' (v.18). Both men asked the same question of the Angel of the Lord and significantly, both men received the same answer, a counter-question as to why they asked for the name of God. It is worth noting that this withholding of God's name was by no means conclusive or final. It warned against unseemly intrusion but left the way open for God to reveal himself in other ways and at other times. In fact, it struck a happy balance between divine reserve and divine revelation.

The fact is that God was telling them they were not ready for the full revelation of himself; 'it is secret'. There is in Scripture progressive revelation. God was not going to reveal himself fully until he revealed himself in Jesus Christ, and the day of that revelation was a long way off. It was to come only when the Son actually took a human nature into lasting union

112

with himself — so made it his that it would be written that 'the Word was made flesh, and dwelt among us, (and we beheld his glory, the glory as of the only begotten of the Father,) full of grace and truth' (John 1:14). Only when he had come would the revelation be complete; it was the Son clothed in our human nature who said to men, 'He that hath seen me hath seen the Father' (John 14:9). Thus, despite the fact that Jacob's desire was a good one, the Lord does not grant it because the time had not yet come for full revelation.

Some commentators have suggested that there is a sense of the Angel's displeasure in evidence here. Indeed, the opposite is true. The moment of blessing follows hard upon the counter-question and is an indication of the Lord's pleasure rather than his censure. In the Psalms and the Prophets, it is clear that one of the signs of people being blessed, or not being blessed, is that they 'know', or 'call upon', or do not know or call upon, the Lord's name (cf. Psalms 91:14; 99:6; Isaiah 64:7). Martin Luther saw in this refusal to name himself God's desire that the whole experience should, to some extent, retain its mystery, and that Jacob should be made to progress in his knowledge of God through new experience and constant prayer and reflection.

Final revelation

We live in the clear light of the gospel. We know the one who fully reveals God. Although this is so, we are not able to say that we know all about him; there is still much of him for us to know. We know his name: 'Thou shalt call his name JESUS: for he shall save his people from their sins' (Matthew 1:21). We know his mission: he came to glorify the Father's name and save those the Father loved (John 17:4-7), and we also know that God has exalted his name high over all (Philippians 2:9). It was the name which became despised among the elders and the rulers of Israel, and ever after identified with rejection and crucifixion. But it is also for ever identified with salvation from sin, with the grace and mercy of God, and with the inward peace of God's people. It is exalted in heaven, and it is exalted in the heart of every true Christian. The decree of the Father is 'that at the name of Jesus every knee should bow' (Philippians 2:10).

Jacob could not know that fuller revelation at this stage in God's redemptive programme, but his question expressed a desire which is the desire of all regenerate men — to know more of God and his nature, that is all that his name represents. As soon as we know Jesus we want to know more of him. The moment Jacob had the Angel in his hands, he wanted to know more of him. Says John Calvin, 'It is to be observed, that although Jacob piously desires to know God more fully, yet, because he is carried beyond the bounds prescribed to the age in which he lived, he suffers a repulse: for the Lord, cutting short his wish, commands him to rest contented with his own blessing' (*Genesis*, p.201). God did not reveal to Jacob those aspects of his character which would be made clear, finally, only in Christ's coming, but he 'blessed him there' (v.29). We can be sure that if we long to know more of God he will bless us.

The power of love

The rule of God is in one sense a terribly solemnizing thought. When it first comes home to our hearts it is even frightening. What we must do in the face of that fear is remember this: the rule of God is the rule of love, and it is the rule of grace. We must not lose sight of the fact that it is always the submission of love to love. The gospel speaks to every Christian and says, 'One is your Master' (Matthew 23:8). But then, any fear involved in that thought is immediately relieved by the fact of who that master is, 'One is your Master, even Christ.'

Paul is an old Christian writing from prison when he says 'I count all things but loss for the excellency of the knowledge of Christ Jesus my Lord' (Philippians 3:8). If you are an old

Christian that is the great longing of your heart too: to know more about Jesus. 'That I may know him, and the power of his resurrection, and the fellowship of his sufferings, being made conformable unto his death' (v.10). There is a strong measure of that in what Jacob is asking when he calls out, probably still in a voice charged with anguish and tears, 'Tell me, I pray thee, thy name.' God's response is immediate and is a double one: it comes not only in word, but in deed also: 'Wherefore is it that thou dost ask after my name? And he blessed him there.' When God commands, men are blessed; and when God blesses men he reveals himself in the doing of it, and men come to know his love. That lifts the soul on to a new plane of experience and knowledge of God. The power of his grace does what nothing else in all the world can do; it makes God known in actual experience.

When the heavy, unwieldy fishing boats are left high and dry on a beach, nothing can move them except the tide flowing in. When the great power of the flooding tide covers the beach it is capable of floating the heaviest boat, and it lifts it so gently, and floats it so easily, that no strain or danger is involved at all. That is what the love of God in Christ does when it comes into our hearts. It has power to lift our spirits, cleanse our hearts, and move our innermost, stubborn wills, and yet it does it so gently and graciously that life is maintained and the soul is enriched. This is what is involved in the blessing of Jacob.

Last century, the famous Free Church of Scotland leader, Dr Thomas Chalmers, preached one of the world's most celebrated sermons under the title, 'The expulsive power of a new affection'. It centred on this thought of how, when the love of Christ comes into the heart of a sinner, it drives the other, old affections and lusts of life out before it and fills the mind with new thoughts, the heart with new desires.

Where I come from, in Ardnamurchan, Argyllshire, there was a short distance from our house a little crofting village, and there was a lovely little white sandy bay there. Through one of the crofts a stream ran into the bay and when the spring tides were reaching their high-water mark, and running inland at their maximum height, this little stream, which had a flow of lovely fresh water in it, would be completely reversed. The tide would come up over the sands to the edge of the grass, and then rush up the narrow banks of the little stream. It was then that a strange thing happened. The tide pushed the fresh water of the river back on itself, until, two hundred yards upstream, in old John's croft, the water was as salt as the sea far out in the bay. Why? Because it was no longer the stream; it was the sea water. The current of fresh water had been turned in its tracks; the tide of the mighty Atlantic had flooded in and pushed the stream back towards its own source.

That is just an illustration of what the love of God in Christ does when it comes into our hearts. It changes the direction and flow of our lives. It reverses the current. It is not just something that happens only at conversion. It happens again and again. The current in which Jacob's life had been moving was turned into another channel. That happens in conversion. It happens when we come to know Christ as Saviour and then it can happen again and again. The current of our life is being redirected to the source of life, to God himself. This process is called progressive sanctification. 'The path of the just is as the shining light, that shineth more and more unto the perfect day' (Proverbs 4:18).

THE SOVEREIGNTY IN THE ENCOUNTER

Knowing the blessing of God.

While we cannot, and must not, ignore the physical struggle as the Scripture sets it before us, it is the fact of the Angel blessing Jacob which takes the entire encounter beyond the mere circumstance of a wrestling match, or a trial of strength between the two contestants. This is evidenced by the emphasis in the narrative, 'And he blessed him there.' Luther insists that the story of Peniel is an outline account of the dealing of God with his saints, so that in reading it we can trace out the essentials of what God is doing with us, and be prepared for more to come.

There can be no doubt that, in the moment when God blessed him, Jacob knew who his adversary was. In a very real sense, that blessing, with its imparting of divine grace — love, favour, and power — was the Angel's answer to Jacob's question. Thus it ever is, and ever has to be. We cannot understand who God is in all the glory and power of his being. Had the Angel uttered a name, Jacob would not have been capable of understanding all that the name implied of the divine person in whose hands he was held, but what Jacob could not absorb with his mind he could experience in his heart. So it is with ourselves even in this gospel age. We cannot comprehend God. However, in Christ, we can apprehend him! We cannot encompass him with our minds, but we can embrace him in our hearts.

This is really what the Bible means when it talks about a 'blessing'. We can experience God's presence, and know his power, and have the virtue of his grace flow through our beings in cleansing, renewing, uplifting power. That is what a blessing is. It is the imparting of grace. When God gives us his grace he gives us himself, for ultimately, grace cannot be severed or divorced from God. It is power, but it is power that is imparted through the fellowship of another will, another heart, another person. Blessing comes from a personal God and it touches and affects every faculty, every aspect of our personality.

The nature of a true blessing

A blessing, however, is more than that. Where men are truly blessed of God that blessing brings them into a new place of obedience to God and his will. It is vitally important that we

117

grasp this point. Many people imagine that the blessing of God always makes one 'feel good'. It gives a warm glow in the breast; it leaves a singing in the heart; it makes one feel 'uplifted'. These are all replies and definitions that Christians give when asked what they mean when they say that God has 'blessed' them.

Of course, one or all of those feelings may well accompany the blessing of God at any particular time. But equally, they may not! For example, how 'uplifted', or how 'good' did Jacob feel even as the Angel was holding him and blessing him? Furthermore, the bestowal of the blessing on Jacob incorporates not just that particular moment but the whole process which led up to it. In the best sense of all, the sense of bringing him into humble submission and obedience, God had been 'blessing' the patriarch from the very minute he laid hold of him in the wrestlers' catch. But, and this is the point to be driven home to our hearts, not every moment of that encounter 'felt good' to Jacob. The blessing of God may well be a very painful, hard, wounding experience, as indeed it had been for Jacob through the progress of the long night. What will ultimately prove any experience of a spiritual kind to be a true blessing of God's grace is whether it issues in renewed love and obedience.

Perhaps you have been a Christian for a long time, or perhaps you are not a Christian yet at all. It may be that your thoughts are confused, and that you are striving and wrestling against the promptings of God's Holy Spirit, resisting the efforts of the Angel who is Christ the Lord. Many Christians have been where you are now as they sought God's blessing. That is where Jacob found himself. The only way to find peace from all these strivings and contentions of your mind and heart is to do as Jacob did: submit yourself totally to the hands of Jesus. Here, you have an advantage over Jacob. You know, as he did not, that these hands are hands which were wounded for our sins.

THE SALVATION IN THE ENCOUNTER

Now we come to the words of verse 30, and the thought here is exceptionally beautiful: 'And Jacob called the name of the place Peniel: for I have seen God face to face, and my life is preserved.' What sort of place was Peniel in the thought of Jacob? What sort of place would it remain in his memory for the years to come?

The place of God's fellowship

This is the reality that the gospel sets before us still. We can still encounter God as Jacob did, in space, in time, in history. In his mighty grace revealed in Christ, and by his Holy Spirit, God can come into, can touch, and can transform our lives so that we are brought into a place of new obedience to him. That is what it means to be a Christian. He is one who seeks, and does, the will of God as it is revealed in God's Word.

'I have seen God face to face.' To help us in our understanding of this momentous phrase, let us consider these words of the apostle John: 'In the beginning was the Word, and the Word was with God' (John 1:1). The Greek term translated 'with God' involves and indicates a sort of movement in the direction of God; it speaks of a relationship between two, a fellowship, a looking 'into' God by the Word. It is William Hendriksen who beautifully translates it like this: 'In the beginning was the Word, and the Word was face to face with God.' Notice the phrase, 'face to face': that means fellowship between the eternal Father and the eternal Son from all eternity. That must be the acme, the very pinnacle of what personal fellowship means. It is the fellowship of person to person communication and living response that is being conveyed to us.

As we allow that thought of what communion and fellowship is to illumine our understanding of what Jacob experienced in encounter with God, we begin to appreciate the awe which filled his soul. He has been admitted into a fellowship that surpasses all other relationships. It is into fellowship with God himself, through the Angel of the covenant, with its blessing and perfection and love that Jacob the twister has been allowed. Indeed, even that is a poor way to express the matter. It is far more wonderful than that, for he has been brought into the warmth of this fellowship by omnipotent grace and eternal love. Jacob has been able to look on God in the face of Jesus pre-incarnate. This is why he says, 'I have seen God face to face.' 'I have had fellowship; a fellowship which has humbled and yet has exalted and transformed me, and has left me no longer Jacob but Israel.' Blessing is from a person to a person. It brings a man into the fellowship of God.

Paul has the very same thought in 2 Corinthians 4:6. 'For God, who commanded the light to shine out of darkness,' — and how that demonstrates his power, his grace, and his holiness — 'hath shined in our hearts, to give the light of the knowledge of the glory of God in the face of Jesus Christ.' It is God who bestows the blessing through Christ the Anointed One, through a personal Mediator. Every blessing that God has ever given to a lost sinner or a saved sinner, he has given because of Jesus and through Jesus.

A lonely place, a place of struggle, of fear, of wounding, of tears — Peniel was all of these. But Peniel would live on in Jacob's mind as the place of blessing. It is a lovely name, compounded of two words. It takes a Hebrew word for 'face', and it links it with one of the great Hebrew names for God — *El* — a name we have already seen as part of Jacob's new name. That Hebrew name for God is one which is expressive of the energy of his being, his power, and his strength. That is the one with whom Jacob came into contact: *El* — the God of power. If there is one thing we need for salvation, transformation, and sanctification of individuals, it is the power of God working with us; and, if we are truly

Christ's, we have all the power of omnipotence provided for us and directed through one channel. All the power of omnipotence is harnessed by love, and it gives us that beautiful, biblical word 'grace'. That is what grace is: omnipotence harnessed by love.

The place of God's favour

In gratitude for the mercy in this experience, Jacob marked the spot for all time with one of the loveliest names in the Old Testament. Peniel, the face of God. There is a significant use of the word 'face' right through the narrative. In verse 20, where Jacob says he will appease Esau, the Hebrew literally translates to 'cover over his face', and points to something which happens between people where guilt has intervened and threatens fellowship. In relation to God it is used for the thought of atonement — a 'covering over' of sin so as to hide it from God's face. The consequence of covering the face is that the person no longer sees the guilt. This is what Jacob is saying when he speaks of appeasing Esau. His own guilt, and especially the enmity it has aroused, is in the forefront of his thought.

Jacob's words that he would appease Esau with the 'present that goeth before', also involve the thought of its going before his 'face'. He says, '. . . and afterward I will see his face'; but would it be in peace or in anger? It is then that he adds, 'peradventure he will accept of me', which literally translated reads, 'lift up his face', that is, forgive him. The gist of verse 20, then, is that Jacob trusts that his gift will enable him to meet Esau face to face, and that in that meeting Esau will forgive him, or show himself gracious to him. The words Jacob uses, and especially the word 'appease', highlight the gravity of the meeting. It is going to involve coming face to face with a wounded, dangerous foe. But Jacob will remember that he comes face to face with Esau, having survived coming face to face with God.

The place of God's forgiveness

The words of Jacob as he contemplated the meeting with Esau not only interpret his fears of Esau but give us an insight into his feelings on leaving Peniel, reflecting on the newly-ended encounter with God. It has been direct and intimate and God has lifted up his face upon him, and shown himself gracious. He has been 'preserved' from the swift justice that his sin deserves. While not stated explicitly, the idea of pardon, forgiveness, gracious reception is in the forefront of his thought as he expresses his sense of wonder at having seen God and lived to tell the tale. What thoughts must have passed through his mind! 'I have been wrestling with God and yet, I am still alive — I have not been destroyed.'

The impact of the encounter is not only one of wonder at the fact that he has had his arms around the Angel of God. Neither is it only that the implication of the face to face encounter meant gracious pardon. It also embodies the thought that seeing God was something that no one survived. But how gracious the Angel had been. For Jacob's protection he had retired with the dawn, and with the sunrise Jacob was once more alone. One wonders if Jacob did not deeply ponder the thought that it was because God came as 'man' that his life had been preserved. Yet the outstanding impression in his mind as he leaves, and names the spot of the encounter, is not that of man, but rather of God. That is the significance of the title he bestows upon it, 'Face of God'. That name reveals to us how deeply he had penetrated the realities of what he had experienced and how precisely he had recognized whose blessing he had enjoyed.

Imagine, generations after that, a little boy walking along with his father and coming to Peniel and saying, 'Dad, why is it called Peniel, the face of God?' 'Ah, well, my son, it is called Peniel because here God met with our great father Jacob. Jacob was never the same again, and he wanted us, his children, to know that men can meet with God.' In a sense, the whole incident can be summarized for us, as for Jacob, in that simple thought. Encounter involves meeting with God and living to tell of it, though sinful nature should perish at so holy a contact.

Jacob's final reflection as we have it here, 'and my life is preserved', is not merely a negative, but rather a positive statement. God did more than save Jacob from harm, he restored him into a place of favour and strength. Salvation is never merely 'from', it is always 'to' as well; it is never merely negative, it is positive. Restored as he was, forgiven by God as he now knew himself to be, Jacob is ready to go and meet with Esau. Because he had seen God face to face he could go to meet his brother knowing that he could look him directly in the eye. Leaving Peniel he is no longer merely 'Jacob'; he is 'Israel' as well.

8

*'And as he passed over Penuel the sun rose
upon him, and he halted upon his thigh'*
(Genesis 32:31).

What a moving picture those words paint for us! The long,
lonely night of pain, anguish, and conflict is over and the
light of a new day has arrived. The sun is rising upon Jacob,
and as he leaves the place to which he had come in solitude
and darkness, he does so in all the glow of a fresh blessing
from God. The words form a fitting conclusion to these
chapters for they gather up the events that took place at
Peniel and indicate the issue of those events in the personal
experience of Jacob.

'The sun rose upon him.' He goes from Peniel in the light
and knowledge of a fresh experience of God's grace. That
grace has enabled him to prevail with the Lord, and has given
him a new confidence that the Lord will achieve his covenant
purposes and fulfil his covenant promises. However, that is
not the entire picture. There is a contrast drawn on the
natural and physical level. The splendour and glory of the
new day highlight Jacob's recent bodily weakness as he leaves
the place of encounter behind; 'he halted upon his thigh'. The
deeply but beautifully drawn contrast on this level of the visible and the temporal points us on to the great paradox on the
level of the invisible and the eternal. Together they testify to
the fact that Jacob has been blessed.

Jacob has 'had power over the angel', but in that conquest
has had his pride and self-confidence put 'out of joint'. He

has been taught in no uncertain fashion that the place of spiritual weakness is, in the economy of grace, the only place of spiritual strength. Those words at the head of this chapter relate the experience of 'Jacob' in the watches of the night to the emergence of the new man 'Israel' in the dawning of the day. In this way they summarize the significance of the experience for us. The place, named now; the light, risen now; the man, limping now — those realities, caught in three little phrases, tell us who was the real winner of this wrestling encounter. The Angel who initiated it, who dictated its course, who ensured its outcome, has achieved a marvellous spiritual advance in the heart of Jacob. Jacob has been conquered, but has demonstrated a persistence which owed itself to the help of God, and which culminated in the sort of submission that only grace can bring about.

Let us examine the text, then, and gather up the lessons it contains.

THE NAME THAT ENSHRINED THE BLESSING

Once more there is an emphasis upon the name which Jacob has given the spot — Penuel is just another form of the name Peniel — and fittingly so. In his naming of this place Jacob left a monument to generations yet to come, marking the place not only for himself in future days, but for the instruction of his posterity. The name of Peniel would leave a lasting testimony that God had appeared there and that Jacob had been blessed. This was to be more than a private revelation of God to one individual; it was to have relevance and importance for the church in the ages yet to come.

We have already seen the importance of places not only in the life of Jacob but in the experience of God's people in every age. There are places which are dear to the Lord's people. These are the places where God met with them, where eternity came down into time, and life was transformed, and

God was made known and became loved. It is the most important factor in life for any one of us — that we have a place which has been a place of blessing to our souls as Peniel was to the soul of Jacob.

The place names in Israel all have significance. Beersheba, Bethel and those other beautiful names all point to something that God did for his people. I remember conversing with a lovely old Christian on the island of Lewis and he started talking about times of revival that he had known when he was a young man in his native village. 'You know, Douglas,' he said, 'there is hardly a stone or a stream or a rock down on the shore but men and women could point to them and say, "There God graciously met with me and there God changed my life."' I am sure that everyone who believes in the Lord Jesus Christ can look back to some place and say, 'Yes, there God met with me in Christ; and because he met with me I called it my "Peniel" — I looked on the face of God and was not destroyed.'

If you are a Christian, I am sure you have done that again and again. Encourage your soul in this way. When did you last have a place to which you could point and say, 'God met me afresh and my life has never been the same again. I have been more humble because I was blessed, and I have been more blessed because I was humbled.'

What kind of place was Peniel, this place where God met with Jacob, the place that was to perpetuate the memory of this gracious visitation? In what kind of place will God be pleased to meet with you? Peniel had significant associations for Jacob.

A place of prayer

It was primarily a place of prayer. Peniel is one of the places in God's Word where we have profound teaching upon the importance of prayer.

We have seen from Hosea that prayer is a central feature of

the whole episode. We know from him that it was God who was involved with Jacob at Peniel. Jacob must have known that the same person had appeared to Abraham, accompanied by two angels (Genesis 18:1-22), and that he was the same Lord who had revealed himself at Bethel. Scripture recounts several appearances of this one who is called, variously, the Angel of the covenant, or the Messenger of the covenant, or the Mediator of the covenant — they all indicate the coming, or the presence, of the same person — the one who wrestled with Jacob.

Peniel illustrates that it is God's presence with us that makes a place of prayer. That, in turn, teaches us that prayer itself can be a very varied, and variable, experience simply because it involves a living relationship with the Lord. Christian believers sometimes are engaged in prayer that means conflict and wrestling and touching and breaking and humbling. Can we ever be in the presence, the majestic presence, of the Eternal One and not feel that we are dust? Can we ever be there in communion and fellowship with him and entertain pride in ourselves or our doings? There will be times in prayer when we are made conscious of the feeble limits of our thought in the presence of the infinitely wise, aware of our vile hearts in the presence of the infinitely holy. There will also be times of rich blessing in our exercise of prayer. Prayer does not guarantee blessing; prayer does not guarantee salvation; but salvation and blessing are bound together with prayer.

It was the godly Bishop Ryle who said that God has no dumb children, and it is impossible to understand anyone who expects to obtain and to maintain the blessing of God without a place of prayer in his or her life. The great Christian men that we talk about from the past: John Elias and Daniel Rowland of Wales, Charles Spurgeon of London, Whitefield and Wesley, Calvin and Luther; and the great men of the Scottish revivals, John Livingstone at Kirk O'Shotts, Robert

Murray M'Cheyne in Dundee, William Chalmers Burns at Kilsyth, John MacDonald of Ferintosh, used so powerfully of God throughout the Highlands, men upon whom the power of God rested in unusual measure, and who were mightily blessed in their churches and their communities; these were men, every single one of them, who knew a place of prayer in their lives.

So often we pay lip-service to the practice of prayer. Any one of these men I mentioned — John Elias, or M'Cheyne, or Spurgeon, or Whitefield — was a man of prayer. Martyn Lloyd-Jones was also a man of prayer; we do not hear very much about that, but he never accomplished under God what he did without asking God to do it. This highlights a rather sad tendency amongst us as preachers; we fall into the snare of aping the great men of the pulpit; speaking in the way they spoke, acting in the way they acted, and preaching in the way they preached. We miss the mark simply because we do not have the power, or the presence, of God won in the place of prayer, that made those men what they were.

There is a place for prayer in every place of blessing, and not just for preachers, either. Young people, learn to pray when you are young, and turn prayer into the habit of a lifetime. It is something that demands work and wrestling, and if you think it is going to be easy, you are wrong. You will need all the grace that God can give you to maintain a life of prayer. I have never met one person, young or old, who has backslidden in the Christian life who has not confessed when the hour of honesty came that the sin of backsliding began with the neglect of prayer. If your life is cold, and barren, and bereft of the fellowship of God, there is only one thing to do: get back to God in prayer. It will be a place of pain. Remember how the pride of Jacob prevailed throughout his believing life until this night at Peniel; and then God touched him in the place of his pride and strength so that the selfhood of Jacob was broken. That has to happen, in a measure at least, with every one of us.

A place of penitence

A place of prayer is ever a place of penitence. Penitence is not something that belongs only to the moment of regeneration and of conversion. It is an experience that continues and deepens throughout life. There is great joy in the Christian life, but as long as we have within us the remnants of sin and an evil heart of unbelief, there will be a sense of our own unworthiness, and daily there will be the renewed need to repent and turn again to God. We recall two things which spoke of penitence in the events of Peniel.

At Peniel, Jacob's thigh was touched, his self-confidence was broken, and he was hurt in the one place that a wrestler needs to use in overcoming his opponent. He was rendered helpless; all he could do was turn to God and cling. That is of the very essence of what repentance is. The second factor that told us that there was penitence in this Peniel experience was this. God said to him, 'What is thy name?' and he could not now say as he had said to his father, 'I am Esau; give me the blessing.' He could only look into the eyes of God and say, 'I am Jacob, the twister, the one who needs a new heart and a right spirit.' Those are the two features which made Peniel a place of penitence.

The place of penitence is a very lovely place to be because it links the soul very closely to heaven, and to Christ's work there. It is in penitence that the face of God is made known to us in Jesus Christ. He is ascended up on high. Why? What is his ministry there? One important aspect of it has to do with the repentance of sinners. The testimony of the apostles concerning this should not be overlooked. 'Him hath God exalted with his right hand to be a Prince and a Saviour, for to give repentance to Israel, and forgiveness of sins' (Acts 5:31). That is where all saving repentance comes from. It has its origins in the ministry of the risen Christ. By his Spirit he gives men the power and disposition to repent. The repentance which works in the hearts of God's people is, first of all, a gift of the exalted Saviour before it shows as the grace of the turning life.

In our day we seldom hear or read much about the grace of repentance, and certainly this particular aspect of it is not often preached. The Bible is clear and specific on the matter. One reason why Christ is there on the right hand of God is 'to give repentance . . . and forgiveness of sins', and those two are always linked together. There is never forgiveness apart from repentance. It is understood by all that only God can forgive sin; but let the complementary truth also be clear — if Jesus Christ does not grant you true repentance and a turning to God, you will be lost for evermore.

Because of the kind of gospel which is in vogue in our day you may think that you are doing God a favour by 'deciding for Jesus', to use the most current phrase. But think about that in the light of this experience of Jacob. Is mere mental decision to be equated with biblical repentance? Does God do the sinner the favour in salvation, or is it the sinner who does God the favour by 'deciding for Jesus'? What a blasphemy is in that thought! The biblical facts indicate another story altogether. You need God! You need Christ, and you need repentance or you are for ever lost. Make no mistake about it. Dare you go on without Christ, and without knowing that you are safe in the hands of Jesus? The gospel offer will not always be ours; therefore we should never despise it.

> *There comes a time, we know not when,*
> *A place, we know not where,*
> *That seals the destiny of men*
> *For glory or despair.*

Will the things you now put before the salvation of your soul really be worth the danger of losing it? Will anything be worth while if you are eternally lost? The abiding sting of your hell then will be this, that a Saviour held out his wounded hands in the sincerity of the gospel call and, for a pleasure or a prejudice or a pride of some kind you turned away. May the grace of God, who alone can bring us to repentance, work mightily in us.

A place of perception

Peniel is also a place of perception. Jacob saw God as he had never seen him before. He began to understand God and trust God as he had never done before. We know that seeing God face to face is indicative of fellowship; but it testifies to more than mere fellowship, no matter how wonderful that, in and of itself, may be.

We noticed earlier how Hendriksen translated that great, illuminating statement of John 1:1; 'In the beginning was the Word, and the Word was face to face with God, and the Word was God.' Hendriksen's translation brings out a thought which we might otherwise very easily miss in our English version. It was not just that there was fellowship there between Father and Son; there was also that which was the very basis of the fellowship. There was Sonship in the fellowship, a Sonship recognized and acknowledged and consummated in fellowship. Equally there was Fatherhood in it. Fatherhood recognized and enjoyed, determining and defining the eternal, unchanging quality of the fellowship within Godhead. God is not, and never was, 'alone'. In the Trinity of his persons there has always been fellowship.

This marvellous fact, which underlies and is reflected in the salvation of God's people, finds its counterpart in the experience of Jacob. Because of sin he finds himself 'alone', as we all do, in the great crises of life. Peniel teaches him that this consequence of sin is abolished in the saving, covenant purpose of God. He learns that salvation ushers him into 'face to face' fellowship with God. So the relationship enjoyed by the Saviour is extended by the Spirit of adoption to every believer; in Christ we, too, are made sons of God.

Christ came into this world to win a family for God, and we

131

are the sons of God. Old people, young people — live like sons; live like sons of God; rejoice like sons of God; and sometimes mourn like sons of God; pray like sons of God. Ministers, preach like sons of God. Stop worrying about what your hearers may think of you, and aim to set God before your people. Do not rest content until he has worked in them by his Spirit, and brought them into the family. What does it matter what men think of you? We have to render our account to God, and that will be solemn for every preacher.

THE PERSON WHO BESTOWS THE BLESSING

The supreme impression Peniel left in the memory of Jacob after this was that there he had 'seen God'. 'The face of God', that lovely name by which the spot was to be known, encapsulates the very heart of Jacob's conflict. It was to be the phrase in which the spiritual experience of God's people in every age could be expressed. We find, for example, that it is a phrase God uses to encourage prayer and trust in the soul of the psalmist, and to which David responds in a very humble and touching way: 'When thou saidst, Seek ye my face; my heart said unto thee, Thy face, LORD, will I seek' (Psalm 27:8). It is plain that Jacob places great emphasis on this; he gives us, not only an exposition of the name but the reason for its bestowal: 'for I have seen God face to face'. Questions have been raised on this point of Jacob's seeing God, to which we must turn.

The mystery of God

In the book of Exodus there is a fascinating transaction between God and his servant, Moses. We read, 'And the LORD said unto Moses, I will do this thing also that thou hast spoken: for thou hast found grace in my sight, and I know thee by name. And he said, I beseech thee, shew me thy glory' (Exodus 33:17,18). What a magnificent request! It makes us

132

wonder if we have begun to know how to pray. Do we ask much? Do we ever say, 'O God, show me thy glory'? Then, God speaks again: 'And he said, I will make all my goodness pass before thee, and I will proclaim' — and this is what the goodness of God is — 'I will proclaim the name of the LORD before thee'. Although he is being gracious, he goes on to show Moses that he is being sovereign even in his grace, for he is God, 'and will be gracious to whom I will be gracious, and will shew mercy on whom I will shew mercy. And he said, Thou canst not see my face: for there shall no man see me, and live' (vv. 19,20). What was the lesson Moses was being taught? Simply this; sinful man cannot look on the face of the Almighty and survive.

No one can behold the essential glory of God. He is the invisible God; he is the God who dwells in the midst of light and of glory inaccessible. Let that be uppermost in your mind when you are on your knees. Remember the kind of God he is. Of course, the gospel tells us that we have access to this God in the man Christ Jesus; in him we look up and say, 'Our Father which art in heaven', but the Father who is in heaven is still the God who dwells in the midst of everlasting light. Therefore the question of Isaiah, 'Who among us shall dwell with the devouring fire? who among us shall dwell with everlasting burnings?' (Isaiah 33:14), is still one to grapple with. So is his answer as it points onwards to Jesus, 'He that walketh righteously, and speaketh uprightly . . . he shall dwell on high' (vv. 15,16).

Nevertheless, God is gracious. 'You cannot look at my face, Moses, it would destroy you. You are a sinner, but I have prepared and I have planned. I have opened a cleft in the rock.' So speaks grace. 'And the LORD said, Behold, there is a place by me and thou shalt stand upon a rock: and it shall come to pass, while my glory passeth by, that I will put thee in a clift of the rock, and will cover thee with my hand' (Exodus 33: 21,22). God had provided that place himself and it foreshadowed another place which is 'by' God, the place to which he has exalted his Son in our nature. Of him the Bible says, 'who . . . when he had by himself purged our sins, sat down on the right hand of the Majesty on high' (Hebrews 1:3). There is only one refuge for a sinner before a holy God, and that is the rock which was cleft for us on Calvary. When God saves us he takes us and puts us tenderly into the 'riven' Christ, just as he put Moses into the 'clift of the rock', and he covers us with his hand while he passes by. 'But my face', he says to Moses, 'shall not be seen' (Exodus 33:23).

The manifestation of God

Interesting light is shed on this matter by the apostle John. 'In the beginning was the Word, and the Word was with God, and the Word was God . . . And the Word was made flesh, and dwelt among us, (and we beheld his glory, the glory as of the only begotten of the Father,) full of grace and truth . . . No man hath seen God at any time; the only begotten Son, which is in the bosom of the Father, he hath declared (manifested, revealed) him' (John 1:1,14,18). The Son has shown the Father to the world. If you want to know what God is like, look at the Lord Jesus. 'He that hath seen me hath seen the Father; and how sayest thou then, Shew us the Father?' (John 14:9). Here, in the words of the apostle Paul, is 'the mystery of godliness: God was manifest in the flesh' (1 Timothy 3:16).

Professor Finlayson reminded us in the class when he was lecturing on the incarnation, 'Gentlemen, let us never forget that when the Son of God veiled his glory in human nature, he veiled it not in order to conceal but to reveal his deity.' So here with Jacob, God unveiled himself in the form of a real man, making himself visible, tangible, and powerfully present to the patriarch.

The mercy of God

As we have seen from Hosea, this encounter brought tears, weeping, and crying into the supplications of Jacob. It is truly remarkable that the Saviour, the Angel who wrestled with him, entered that same night into an arena of pain and prayer that he was later to know for himself in the very shadow of the cross. The Angel who was wrestling there at Peniel, and who had a weeping, praying, struggling Jacob in his hands — that same one was to go to a garden, emblem of blessing and emblem of curse, and in that garden of Gethsemane his sweat was to be 'as it were great drops of blood' as he agonized before the Father. His prayers also, like those of Jacob, were wonderfully answered. This is written of him: 'Who in the days of his flesh, when he had offered up prayers and supplications with strong crying and tears unto him that was able to save him from death, and was heard in that he feared (trusted)' (Hebrews 5:7).

How amazing that this very experience which Jacob knew in the Angel's hands, the Son was to know in the Father's hands in the days of his flesh! How wonderful that 'in all things it behoved him to be made like unto his brethren'! (Hebrews 2:17) Following Jesus, you will not put a foot on any spot where the foot of Jesus has not already been. He has been made like us in all things with one exception, and it is a great and blessed exception — 'yet without sin' (Hebrews 4:15). That makes him a Saviour.

THE GLORY THAT EPITOMIZED THE BLESSING

The words in the text above this chapter strikingly and graphically express the blessing in its inward, spiritual reality.

At my boyhood home, on the west coast of Scotland, we have very impressive sunsets. I was brought up and worked for many years on the most westerly point of the British mainland, Ardnamurchan Point. Sometimes, fishing off the

Point in my teenage years on an early summer's evening, or in the hills working my sheep, I found the colours in the sky almost unbelievable. The mountain peaks on the islands which dotted the horizon westwards, would stand out in a blaze of crimson and red, and the sea and the land would fill with a hazy, golden glow. The depth and richness of it all can scarcely be imagined, far less described. Those were unforgettable occasions, which could strike awe into the soul of a pagan, and they often did — my own, in pre-conversion days!

Dawn, and the promise of a new day

Sunsets are beautiful, colourful sights. People came from miles around to see these spectacular phenomena we had through from June until August. There was something that was even more breathtaking but which few people ever saw, and that was the sun rising. What a marvellous thing a new day is. For a Christian each new day brings new experiences of the Lord's love, grace, care — and discipline. It also brings new opportunities, new responsibilities, and new areas of Christian service and Christian witness. This dawn in the life of Jacob testifies to a new day of walking forth with God, and in the light of his blessing.

At lambing time on our farm the rising sun could be astonishingly lovely. Sometimes it could be so special that one knew exactly why it is written that 'God saw the light, that it was good' (Genesis 1:4). From the hills on which I was shepherding, the first image the growing dawn separated from the darkness of night was that of Ben Nevis, the highest mountain peak in Britain. Perhaps 75 miles distant, its majestic outline would begin to stand out in the light of the rising sun, its huge shoulder dominating the mountain ranges that stood between. When its mass became visible, daylight was very near. The lesser peaks would soon be seen.

When the 'Sun of righteousness' (Malachi 4:2) begins to rise upon us, as here with Jacob, events follow a similar pattern. It is the great mountain peak of the eternity and the holiness of God which first fills the horizon, and then other peaks appear, smaller, gentler ones — grace, mercy, goodness — until at last you can see a whole range of mountain tops. The valleys remain dark. Then, as the sun really comes over the horizon and up behind Ben Nevis, so to speak, even the valleys clear. What is happening? The day is breaking. When the dawn breaks 'the shadows flee away' (Song of Solomon 2:17).

Dawn carries exciting prospects with it, the prospects of a new day. These beckon Jacob as he leaves Peniel. As the 'sun rose upon him' it was a symbol of the hope and promise of what a new day holds. A new era in his spiritual history begins to unfold with each step. There are few things more exhilarating, more encouraging, in life than the prospect and promise of a heart into which the light and glory of the gospel have come. What may not God do with such a life; a life newly blessed, newly humbled, newly broken, newly submitted into his hands! That is one of the truly exciting things about a conversion experience. It embraces all the promise of a new day. No wonder the sun shone upon Jacob.

Dawn, and the peace of a new day

When God touches and transforms us in conversion, and then in these great, ongoing experiences of progressive sanctification brings us a new sunrise, we see more of the glory of God, and more of the shadows fly away. Where does this saving work of God all culminate? In perfect light. Where is the inheritance of the saints? In light. 'For there shall be no night there' (Revelation 21:25). A day will dawn and break upon our souls which will be the final dawning for us because it is eternal day. No more darkness; no more sin; no more death; no more tears.

Jacob persevered. He wrestled all through the long hours of darkness, and did not yield until the coming dawn made the

Angel-antagonist take a new line of approach with him. Now he was enjoying the blessing of God as he walked away from Peniel, but we dare not forget how and when it had all started. It had begun in the dark — in a spiritual as well as a physical sense — and it had ended only with the coming of light.

Sometimes sunsets can be very disturbing, but the sunrise always brings a soothing sense of tranquillity and peace with it. That sense of sheer peace comes through very vividly from the words before us. The spiritual truth presented here is probably familiar to you from the words of one of the ancient Scottish Paraphrases on the words of Hosea 6:1-4:

> Long hath the night of sorrow reign'd;
>   The dawn shall bring us light;
> God shall appear, and we shall rise
>   With gladness in his sight.
>
> Our hearts, if God we seek to know,
>   Shall know him, and rejoice;
> His coming like the morn shall be,
>   Like morning songs his voice.

THE TOKEN THAT EXHIBITED THE BLESSING

The final phrase of this verse closes the account of Jacob wrestling at Peniel. As he left the spot, bathed in the growing light of the rising sun, there was something particularly noticeable about him: 'he halted upon his thigh'. That speaks specifically of four things — four things new in the life of this man as the result of encounter with God.

There was *abasing*. This was a strong, self-sufficient, husky man who had never limped in his life. He had been the smart man and no one had ever had the better of him either physically or spiritually. However, the wrestling of the night had brought him a new experience. It had taken him to the place where he wept, and prayed, and clung to God like a little child. That was very humbling; and humbling of the spiritual kind is ever a sore experience. 'What is thy name?' 'Jacob.'

There was *wounding*. Jacob's thigh was out of joint as he wrestled with his opponent. It was a painful experience without a doubt. When God 'touches' the things in our life which are the source of our strength; when he puts them out of joint for us; when we are made to cling to the Lord, and feel just like little children once more, then we know pain of mind and spirit. Faith does not guarantee freedom from those experiences, although it upholds us in them, just as the Angel upheld Jacob.

There was *healing*. Jacob walked away from Peniel. If he had only been wounded he would not have been walking; but he was not only wounded, he was healed. That 'touch' of God had been miraculous, for it wounded and healed all at the same time. This is the truly outstanding feature about the saving grace of God in the lives of his people: it wounds and it heals in the same touch.

There was *marking*. The encounter at Peniel left its mark on Jacob, and it was a mark which was to be seen in him until the end of his days. That mark was left in a place where it would be clearly seen by all who knew him. It would be seen in his daily walk; every step in the future would testify to encounter with God.

CONCLUSION

Thus we come round to morning and light. I always picture this scene by placing myself amongst Jacob's retinue to whom he was returning in that new day. They see immediately the limp in his walk and, I like to think, the light on his face. They cluster round, and they ask the obvious questions. He stills them: No, it was no accident. God met with me; the Lord crippled me and crowned me. I have been mastered, and I am become master. I am no longer just Jacob, I am Israel, for I have prevailed with God; and in him, I will prevail with men also.

Then I look on through the years and I hear the questions of the new generation: 'Dad, why is old grandfather Jacob lame?' 'Oh, my son, that is the mark given by the touch of the Angel, the night that God gripped him, the night that God blessed him. He has been lame ever since, and quite different in his life and covenant obedience. It happened at Peniel.'

A quotation from one of the great Welsh preachers sums up the message of Peniel for us. John Elias wrote these words:

> In some areas where the cause deteriorates or declines, many things are suggested for its renewal not as a means to procure the face of God, but instead of God.

What was John Elias saying? This: the only answer to all our problems in our own personal lives, the only answer to all the problems in our fellowships and congregations, the only answer, ultimately, to all the problems in the churches of Christ on earth is to do as Jacob did: *procure* the face of God.

Let us pray:

Our gracious God, seal thy Word upon our hearts and bless us; and O Eternal One, do for us what we are totally unable to do for ourselves. Lay hold of us, lift us into a new level of obedience and holiness, and when we have made our covenants with thee, help us, O God, to be faithful to them. O God, seal our covenants this day, our covenants between our souls and thee, with the precious blood of Christ. We pray, Lord, that thou wilt cleanse us from all the sins and the disobedience and the failure which are ours, and give us to know new obedience, new triumph, new victory, in our walk with God. Hear

140

us, O Lord, and answer us in the majesty of thy grace and in the tenderness of thy mercy, for we ask it all, with cleansing and pardon, in the all-prevailing name of Jesus, for his sake and glory. And now unto thee, Father, Son, and Holy Spirit, we would ascribe all the honour and the power and the dominion and the might and the majesty, world without end. Amen.

Further titles from the Evangelical Press of Wales

Out of the Depths by D. Martyn Lloyd-Jones. An exposition of Psalm 51 which deals with the problem of human failure and guilt and the divine remedy of repentance.

Why Does God Allow War? by D. Martyn Lloyd-Jones. Biblical teaching on how Christians should face evil and suffering.

Truth Unchanged, Unchanging by D. Martyn Lloyd-Jones. A powerful examination of life's fundamental questions, and a penetrating diagnosis of the human condition.

Martyn Lloyd-Jones: The Man and His Books by Frederick & Elizabeth Catherwood. A fascinating personal account of 'the Doctor' by his daughter and son-in-law.

The Holiness of God and of His People by Hugh D. Morgan. A warm, practical application of the Bible's teaching on an all-important subject.

One Bible, One Message? by Bryan A. Williams. This book looks at a number of central truths and clearly demonstrates the complete agreement of the Old and New Testaments on these matters.

God Cares by Brian Edwards. A very practical exposition of Psalm 106.

They Beheld His Glory by Peter Trumper. A thrilling look at the birth of the Saviour through the eyes of some of those intimately involved.

Glory Over Calvary by Peter Trumper. Many new insights in the same style as They Beheld His Glory.

To Bala for a Bible by Elisabeth Williams. The true story of Mary Jones and the beginnings of the Bible Society.

The Welsh Revival of 1904 by Eifion Evans. A thorough but readable study of the 1904 Revival. Foreword by D. M. Lloyd-Jones.

Revival Comes to Wales by Eifion Evans. A moving and thrilling account of the mighty working of God the Holy Spirit in Wales at the time of the 1859 Revival.

Howell Harris and the Dawn of Revival by Richard Bennett. A study of the early spiritual life of Howell Harris and the beginnings of the Great Awakening of the eighteenth century in Wales.

'Excuse Me, Mr Davies – Hallelujah!' by Geraint D. Fielder; foreword by Lady Catherwood. The absorbing story of evangelical student witness in Wales in the twentieth century, a story which includes periods of quite remarkable spiritual blessing.

Christian Family Matters edited by Ian Shaw, foreword by Sir Frederick Catherwood. Clear biblical guidelines by experienced contributors on marriage, parenthood, divorce, adoption and other issues that affect family life.

Social Issues and the Local Church edited by Ian Shaw. Subjects covered include the state, work, education, mission, social welfare and the role of women in the local church.

The Christian Heritage of Welsh Education by R. M. Jones and Gwyn Davies. A bird's -eye view of Christian education in Wales down the centuries.

In the Shadow of Aran by Mari Jones. Stories from farm life in the Welsh mountains which present spiritual truths in a vivid way.

Gospel and Church by Hywel R. Jones. An evangelical evaluation of ecumenical documents on church unity.

Christian Hymns edited by Paul E. G. Cook and Graham Harrison. A comprehensive selection of 901 hymns. The various editions available include a large-type words edition. A lineal index and concordance is also available.

Christian Hymn-writers by Elsie Houghton. A collection of brief biographies of some of the great hymn-writers.

Christian Preachers by Nigel Clifford. A collection of the biographies of some notable preachers.

The Evangelical Magazine of Wales. A bi-monthly magazine with a wide range of articles on all aspects of Christian faith and life.

Christian Handbook by Peter Jeffery. A straightforward guide to the Bible, church history and Christian doctrine.

A SERIES of booklets for the earnest seeker and the new Christian by Peter Jeffery. All are born out of the practical needs of the author's own pastoral work:

Seeking God – for the earnest seeker after faith.

All Things New – a help for those beginning the Christian life.

Walk Worthy – guidelines for those who have just started on the Christian life.

Firm Foundations (with Owen Milton) – a Bible study course introducing new Christians to great chapters of the Bible.

Stand Firm – a young Christian's guide to the armour of God.